ILLUSIONS OF THE MIND
Goan Identity, Migration and Development

ILLUSIONS OF THE MIND
Goan Identity, Migration and Development

by
PRABHAKAR TIMBLE

Research & Editorial Assistance
Akbar Gaded

ILLUSIONS OF THE MIND
Goan Identity, Migration And Development
Prabhakar Timble

© **Prabhakar Timble**

First Edition: 2024

© Published by

Qurate Books Pvt. Ltd.
F-16, Alfran Plaza,
Mahatma Gandhi Road,
Opp. Don Bosco School,
Panaji- Goa 403001
Contact No: 18002106527

www.quratebooks.com

All rights reserved
All rights reserved by author. No part of this publication may be reproduced, stored in a retrieval system or transmitted in any form or by any means, electronic, mechanical, photocopying, recording or otherwise, without the prior permission of the author.

ISBN:978-93-58983-71-5

Printed by Repro

Price : 295/-

*Fondly remembering my dearest Papa,
Shri Narayan Timble.
Seeing my name in print would always
fill his heart with ecstasy.*

Preface

This book which is largely a compilation of my articles in newspapers could have definitely been published much before. It was my obsession that what I write has a limited shelf life that kept me away from venturing into such work.

It was a chance interaction on WhatsApp with Akbar Gaded, a young researcher in Political Science that sparked the beginning. We got in virtual touch during the first phase of COVID-19 with the mutual promise to meet in person only after the publication of the book. He has taken all the pains to surf over 200 writings of mine on the gamut of issues and challenges confronting Goa, finally to select and edit a few. Some writings have been rewritten or modified.

The book is divided into four sections reflecting the core issues so as to make it reader-friendly. The Editor's Word is a good prelude for perusing and understanding the contents.

There is a belief that unless you have a book in print, you are not considered as an author. This maiden publication has seen the light of the day due to the pull and push of my friends' and close relations. My dear friend and well-wisher deeply involved in e-ventures, Frederick Noronha, a journalist and writer pinned the need for documentation on Goa issues. My daughter, Prasanna wants to see me engaged and in public gaze. My wife Smita, gets disturbed as I love to fritter away my time in mundane things. The big push came from Akbar Gaded who took the responsibility of compiling and editing. Left to me, I procrastinate but it was the consistent follow up by Rama Harmalkar and the secretarial assistance of Jonely Godinho from Qurate Books Pvt. Ltd. that finally turned fruitful with this publication. The cover design by Lynessa S. Rodrigues has added value to the book.

I am deeply indebted to all of them including the Editors of all newspapers who published my thoughts in their esteemed columns.

Before I part, I want to say "I was born in a liberal Goa where fellow Goans exhibited empathy and lived in harmony maintaining self-respect and mutual respect. I want to die in this Goa and not one where people are frozen and polarised on grounds of religion, faith and illiberal attitudes".

Prabhakar Timble
8180975518

Editor's Word

"Do not follow where the path may lead. Go instead where there is no path and leave a trail"
Ralph Waldo Emerson

Goa has transitioned from being ruled by Portuguese to becoming the smallest State of India embarking an adventurous journey in all aspects of development, leaving behind a trail of struggle & success for us to cherish forever. This book is an attempt to narrate this story through thematic sections and chapters.

It is with great pleasure that I introduce to you this compelling collection of insightful observations and thought-provoking analyses, which have been originally published in various local dailies, stimulating and encouraging every reader to think critically and engage deeply with distinct perspectives penned by Prof. Prabhakar Timble, a distinguished voice in the realm of socio-political & economic discourse in Goa.

Titled **"Illusions of the mind — Goan Identity, Migration and Development"** encapsulates the essence of Goa through a diverse array of topics, offering a profound exploration of Goa's past, present, and future i.e. from reminiscing the Goan history to dissecting the intricate nuances of contemporary Goan politics and socio-economic landscape.

In his astute reflections spread across multiple sections, Prof. Timble navigates through the nostalgia of Goa's cultural heritage, examines the challenges of transitioning times and critically evaluates the developmental paradigms shaping the state's trajectory to the sobering realities of its present predicaments. Each article invites readers on a journey of introspection.

Amidst the discord of misinformation and socio-political fallacies, there exists an urgent need for awareness and informed dialogue. This book anticipates to serve as a source of information, catalyzing the intellectual discourse and civic engagement to spark intellectual dialogue among the people of Goa.

As I am deeply rooted in the academic and social fabric of Goa, my motivation in editing this anthology stems from a keen belief in the power of knowledge to ignite transformative change. This book will not only be significant for the common man but also academicians and everyone who is interested in understanding Goa's journey.

Compiling these articles presented its own set of unique challenges, particularly in organizing the rich tapestry of insights under distinct thematic sections. By weaving together disparate threads of thought into a cohesive narrative, we aim to offer readers a fresh view of Goa's multifaceted identity and the issues that shape its destiny.

I extend my heartfelt gratitude to Prof. Prabhakar Timble for his invaluable contributions to this endeavor and to the people of Goa whose collective experiences and aspirations serve as the bedrock of this anthology. May this book ignite a spark of introspection, dialogue, and action, paving the way for a more informed and empowered society.

Akbar Gaded
Assistant Professor (Political Science)
Govt. College of Arts, Science & Commerce, Khandola, Goa.

Contents

Section 1. The Nostalgia
1. The Fragrance of Goa 3
2. Opinion Poll: The Event That Shaped Goa's Destiny 6
3. Let Opinion Poll not be a Tomb of Asmitai 15
4. Futureless or Futuristic Agriculture! 18

Section 2. Goa in Transition
5. Small States, Better Governance 23
6. Too much Government, Declining Governance 27
7. Amchem Goem: The Sweet and Sad Chapters 31
8. Goa Needs a Growth Story 34
9. Demography Versus Development 37
10. Opposition to Projects Will Harm Goa--I 40
11. Opposition to Projects Will Harm Goa-II 43
12. The Threat of Negative Activism 47
13. Goa Business DNA 51

Section 3. Developmental Delusions
14. Tourism in Goa: A SWOT Analysis 57
15. Casino Industry, Tourism and Economic Growth 61
16. Casinos: Jackpot or blindness for Goa 64
17. Drugs: Crossing the line of control 67
18. Casino wins, Tourism loses 70
19. Tourism: Regaining The Lost Paradise 73
20. Mining: Breaking the Jinx 76
21. Standing with Melauli-Sattari 84

22. IIT Learning: Making land losers beneficiaries: 87
23. Airport: One Enough, Two Not Yet 90

Section 4. Identity and Migration
24. Selling Impossible Dreams 97
25. Preserving Goa sans special status 101
26. Emigration of the Blue-Collared and Respectable 105
27. Migration: Escape from Poverty 108
28. Migration in Goa: Gains and Concerns 112
29. The Changing Demography of Goa 118
30. The Race for Portuguese Nationality 121
31. Making People Illegal 125
32. Migrants are Assets, not Criminals 128
33. Migrants are people not Demons 131
34. Goans and Migrants: A Changing Discourse. 134
35. Making Peace with Migrants 144
36. Mujhe Ghar Jana Hai 147
37. Goa & Goans: No Integration Deficit 150
38. The Last Word 154

Section 1.

The Nostalgia

> Goa, once under Portuguese decree was liberated on 19th December 1961. It soon began to encounter socio-economic challenges as changes and mainstream politics disturbed the values which Goans espouse and cherish. The readers can relate the feeling of nostalgia on Goa Opinion Poll campaigns and how the spine chilling borderline arithmetic of Goa Opinion Poll 1967 shaped the state of Goa. Furthermore, the author elaborates on how out-migration of Goans in search of better economic opportunities, public investment in infrastructure and private capital locked in industry and service sectors has created a local space of opportunities which are occupied by migrants from neighbouring states who see Goa as a fish on a platter. Undoubtedly, Goa is developing. Is it losing its intrinsic fragrance?

In this my land of Goa,
Pain is sweeter than pleasure,
My whole life is attached,
The fragrance of my poems fan
Out completely only from there

(Poet B.B. Borkar fondly known as Bakibab)

The Fragrance of Goa

Just 15 lakhs, relatively tolerant vis-à-vis the rest of India, welcomes each and everybody, good beaches and pious countryside, social harmony despite deliberate efforts by politicians and saffron leaders to disturb and distort, instantly likeable communities due to open attitudes and non-bothering nature of people, but under the clutches of highly unstable and greedy politicians is how Goa could be described today.

Going by the economic indices of investment, per capita income, and basic infrastructure, this small territory is far above the national average. The Human Development Index (HDI) in terms of literacy, primary health care, social harmony, women empowerment and agreeable environment is anybody's envy. And added to this is the tradition of Goan hospitality, a lifestyle where work and zest of living naturally blends, a culture of concern, love and warmth without expectation. Putting a limit and saying enough to need as well as to greed comes spontaneously to a Goan. These are the same reasons why Goans are tied to Goa, why Indians crave for shelter and neighbourhood in Goa and also why foreigners find this damsel attractive.

Today, this fragrance is under attack. Goa is caught in the web of reckless economic growth and valueless politics. With political decline, social regress, environmental negligence, cultural negativism and identity threats, Goans are in a dilemma.

Immigration has proved to be good for the development of the State. It has provided skilled and unskilled manpower required for the different sectors of the economy. But, further immigration at the same pace would disturb the balance and opportunities for locals. Migration of Goans in other parts of the country and overseas has also boosted the local economy in terms of purchasing power. However, we now need positive steps to create opportunities in the State for the educated youth to curb involuntary migration.

The stakeholder here is the local population who are tied to the soil permanently. There are immigrants from neighbouring States who came for making a living and made Goa their home. They found here water, shelter and peace and do not desire to shift. The third segment is the educated youth who migrated to other parts for education or employment and who desire to return home if opportunities knock. These are the three segments which will contribute to the Goa of the future. It is noted with remorse that Goa has little to gain and more to lose from the Overseas Goans descending to Goa for purely year-end breaks or retired bureaucrats of All-India-Services for whom Goa is merely an old age or holiday destination. Added to this, are land bankers who come to buy and sell Goa and for whom Goa is a "commodity" to make a quick buck. The natural fragrance, social harmony and the special identity as reflected through language and lifestyle are no longer safe.

The crying need in Goa is for enlightened leadership in social and political field. Even assuming corruption as the price of development, limitless greed of the few whom we have thrown up in our legislature and local bodies should not remain as an unanswered question.

There are few who still talk about Goans as having not totally mingled into Indian culture or mainstream. Such groups should first learn to understand culture. Jawaharlal Nehru in his Glimpses of World History says *"Culture and civilisation are difficult to define, and I shall not try to define them. But among the many things that culture includes are, certainly restraint over oneself and consideration of others. If a person has not got this self-restraint and has no consideration for others, one can certainly say that he is uncultured."* This is a singular trait in the fragrance of Goa which is worth exporting to the other States of the Indian Union and even to the developed parts of the world. If culture means our behaviour with others, if culture means rejecting discriminatory practices and adopting progressive values, if culture also includes universal values, then Goa and Goans is a storehouse for the national mainstream to draw to its kitty.

When Goans reminiscence the past, it is only in terms of the beautiful bounty of nature and the strong sense of belonging and togetherness as one community transcending barriers of religious faith. However, the community is as divided today as in the past on the metre of caste.

The feeling of "gross aggregate unhappiness" is because of the different kind of expectations of the local population. The primary expectation of people is a sense of overall contentment, well-being, joy and peace, freedom, privacy and communal harmony. These are quite different from the usual economic indicators of growth and availability of material goods and services. This is the distinct fragrance of Goa which invites the bees across boundaries. It would be a deliberate suicide if Goa and Goans attempt to locate commerce in the perfume of drugs, wine, gambling and trafficking in women and children. This is the picture of Goa sold internationally.

We may perceive immediate economic gains but it is a sure road to permanent disablement.

Opinion Poll: The Event That Shaped Goa's Destiny

Let me begin with a quote from the unpublished Ph.D. dissertation of Monte mayor J.M. entitled *"A Sociological Analysis of a Goan village community"*-- 'As a cultural group rooted in the Goan soil, and sharing the same set of traditions, all Goans, whether they are Hindus, Christians, Muslims, all recognize a common oneness that distinguishes them from others on the Indian subcontinent'.

January 19, 1967. I was 11 years old, totally ignorant of the implications of the Opinion Poll or the significance of the outcome, which was celebrated as the Victory Day. I can only recollect the period of campaigning when four-wheelers used to descend on our village with loudspeakers blaring out *"Amchem Goem, Amkam Zai", "Zalach Pahije", "Tumchem Mot-Don panak, "Sang re bhaie, Sang re Tai Muth Konala-Muth Fulala"; "Amkam naka shrikhandpuri, amchi shith-koddich bori."* That time, we used to run after all the vehicles and shout all the slogans, unmindful of the consequences.

Today, the very thought of Opinion Poll sends a chill down my spine. Fortunately, 54.20% voted against merger with Maharashtra. Goa remained a separate territory and was later conferred statehood. The thought of different arithmetic on this day, 57 years ago, is frightening.

Who won and who lost? Is it a victory of anti- merger forces over the Goans propagating merger? Is it a defeat of the Maharashtrian expansionist tendencies? Is it a victory of Konkani over Marathi? Is it a victory of Catholics and a few Hindus over the Hindu Bahujan Samaj? As I see the whole exercise today, I confidently say that it is victory "for" all Goans, though may not be "by" all Goans. All Goans, including those who supported merger, got the opportunity to preserve, protect and promote Goan identity, language and culture. All Goans got the opportunity of self- government and participative democracy in real terms. All Goans could assert the right of locals on local resources. All Goans won, nobody lost.

Historic

The Goa Opinion poll is historic. It was the first poll conducted within the framework of the Indian Constitution to decide a political dispute. It was the first such poll conducted in Bharat after 'Swaraj'. However, an opinion poll was also held in case of princely State of Junagadh, to decide on joining the Indian Union.

In 1955, Prime Minister Nehru had assured the people of Goa that, Goa would be maintained as separate democratic unit. In 1963, at the Jaipur conference of the Indian National Congress, the Prime Minister had stated that the merger of Goa with any neighbouring State is not desirable. The Congress Parliamentary Board passed a resolution to this effect in April, 1964. The debate on the Goa Opinion Poll Bill in Parliament brought a bitter duel between pro-Maharashtra and pro-Mysore members. Nath Pai along with the pro-Maharashtrian members made it clear that linguistically and geographically, Goa should merge. The Mysore lobby was critical of the "pressure tactics" of the Maharashtrian lobby. Jan Sangh leader U. M. Trivedi tried to block the introduction of the bill in the Lok Sabha saying that the matter could be settled by holding elections and there was no need for a separate opinion poll. The Goan MPs, Peter Alvares and Janardhan Shinkre maligned the Anti-Mergerists in Parliament and fixed the coat of pro-Portuguese on Christians. It was Acharya Kripalani who clarified *"I am an Indian and I do not belong to one state. Goans should decide their future."*

It was the first Prime Minister Jawaharlal Nehru who stood firm. There was complete clarity that Goa should not be amalgamated with any adjoining State. To quote Nehru "People of Goa should choose a path of their own choosing". To quote Nehru again: **"We do not intend putting Goa, just as a part of a district of India. We think it is right for Goa to remain a** separate entity in the Union of India and add to the richness of India".

Nehru's maturity and sharpness of the mind even after the results of the first Goa assembly and the Lok Sabha election is commendable. In the 1963 election, the Indian National Congress did not win a single seat in Goa except Daman. The Maharashtrawadi Gomantak Party (MGP) which espoused the cause of merger won 14 seats and the two Lok Sabha seats. Nehru said that the issue of the status of Goa is separate and clearly communicated that the same should not be mixed with the Goa assembly elections.

After the results, the stand of Pandit Nehru did not change. He said, which party won the majority and formed the government does not matter. The original pledge continues. In a letter to Purshottam Kakodkar, Nehru writes "Merger of Goa is not desirable despite the results of election. Government of India is not going to agree to the merger".

Arguments for Merger

Both the camps used and misused religion, caste, culture, nationalism and language to bolster their stands. Those espousing the cause of merger stated that since the states under the Indian Union are reorganized on linguistic basis, Goa is a part of Maharashtra since Marathi is the mother-tongue of Goans and Konkani is its dialect. A. K. Priolkar stated that those who say Konkani is a language are engaging in "parochial patriotism" According to him, Konkani is "Goanese Marathi".

Goa, they claimed has ancestral and religious links with Maharashtra. They also claimed that Maharashtrians started and fought for the liberation of Goa. The seventeen page booklet of the M.G.Party argued that Anti-Mergerists have pre-conceived notions and prejudices. From administrative point of view, the small size of the territory has obstacles. The territory cannot industrially develop on its own. Maharashtra has economic power, finance and enterprise in abundance which can contribute to the development of Goa. The MGP assured complete protection to Konkani and allayed fears of Prohibition of alcoholic breverages.

The Goa Vilinikaran Samiti, the Goa Sahayak Samiti, the Goa-Maharashtra Vilinikaran Agadhi, the Goa-Maharashtra Merger Front, the Goa Socio-cultural Association were of the basic view that Goa does not have separate identity in terms of culture or language. They almost echoed the sentiments of Janardhan Shinkre that those opposed to merger are "not only anti-Maharashtrians but they are anti-Indian and anti- democratic" (Navhind Times dtd 24/11/66). Laximikant Bhembre went further and said "Because a merger now will unleash a tremendous force which will reinforce the national sentiment in repelling the Pakistan and Chinese invaders". This was in keeping with Nath Pai when he said "it was to build a country of united people defended to resist Pakistan aggression and to create a sense of emotional integration that problems like merger of Goa with Maharashtra should be speedily and boldly settled".

The campaigns and meetings used to begin with the "Maharashtra Geet". The fear that separate status would make Goa into another Kashmir or Nagaland and confidence that merger would result in national integration was the common thread in these campaigns. There were appeals to the people of Maharashtra to work and join hands for the merger and volunteers from Maharashtra were actually brought during the time of the opinion poll.

The academic base was provided amongst others by Prabhakar Angle. In an article, (Navhind Times (21/5/65) "Merger-an Inevitability," Shri Angle argued that with merger, there would be economic gains and stated that the Central State Tax would disappear, freight rates would be lowered and the cost of living would come down. He also said that a separate state is not economically viable due to administrative overheads as compared to revenue collections. Stating that the first general election was a verdict in favour of merger, he castigated the

Christian community as having lost touch with Indian culture. Providing statistics of 61.2% Hindus, 36.4% Christians and further clarifying that 3% are Brahmins and 58% are Non-Brahmins, he concluded that merger is inevitable.

Arguments Against Merger

Prof. Armando Menezes was logical when he said *"Merger is denying self-government to Goans. The question before every self-respecting Goan today is: Are we to be conquered once more, in the name of Liberation?"*

The general view of the Council of Action and the other fronts formed was to protect the obliteration of the mother-tongue and the total submersion of the Goan personality. According to the anti-Mergerists, the claim that Goa was always a part of Maharashtra was wanton assassination of elementary history - not only history of Goa but also history of Maharashtra. The second lie is that the language of Goans is Marathi. Prof. Armando Menezes said "We say this lie in excellent Konkani or bad Marathi but whenever two Goans meet, they converse in Konkani or English or Portuguese but never in Marathi".

This group claimed that Goa has a separate identity and demand for statehood is a birth right. Goa has a unique culture, though many feel that Goan culture is western, it is not so. Goa is rich in folk art, folklore and folk music. Goans have a unique lifestyle which is manifested in secular traditions, unique cuisine, festive spirit, trustworthiness, zest for life and a tolerant populace. Nationalism of Goans needs no test. Goans, though a microscopic minority, have excelled in art, architecture, music, philosophy, sports etc. at international levels.

N. J. Bhat argued that Goans have full faith in Indian secularism and it is an insult to Goan nationalism and patriotism if Mergerists say that integration of Goa is not possible. After liberation, Goa need not look at Maharashtra for charity, what we require is self-rule. (Navhind Times dtd. 22/5/65 "Merger not so inevitable"). Commenting on the economic implications of immediate merger, Dr G V. Kamat Helekar (Navhind Times dated 14/1/64) held that the rate of growth of Goa cannot be faster with immediate merger. Maharashtra does not have the capacity to satisfy the needs even if willing and hence under the existing set up the Union government's liberal aid policy can help build the social overheads in Goa".

The Goa Congress and the United Goans Party were committed to independent status. The Goa Congress Meets always demanded democracy and self- rule to Goa and decried attempts to toss Goans like cattle between Maharashtra and Mysore.

Results

317633 Goans exercised their voting right out of the total electorate of 388392 (81.70%). Goa remained a separate territory with 172291 (54.20%) voting against merger.

The first general elections (1963) gave a resounding victory to the Maharashtrawadi Gomantak Party. MGP won in 14 constituencies out of 28, with merger as the main plank in the election manifesto. However, in the opinion poll the Anti-Mergerists got lead in 15 constituencies. In the talukas of Bardez, Mormugao, Salcete and Tiswadi, it was a clean sweep in favour of anti-merger. In the new conquests, in five constituencies, the anti-merger votes were over 45% of the total votes polled, the notable being Sattari wherein it was 49.5%. In areas that were considered as forts of the Mergerists, such as Mandrem, the anti-merger group polled 36% votes. According to Vaman Radhakrishna, this confirmed the defeat of the forces of merger ("Maharashtrawadi Gomantak Pakhsha" - pp.33). Hence, it is not correct to say that anti-merger votes were only from the old conquests due to colonial hangover.

Though the Hindu Bhaujan Samaj largely voted for merger, they cannot be blamed or no motives can be attributed. I tend to agree with the reasoning of Vaman Radhakrishna (MGP-pp.15) when he says that the Bhahujan Samaj felt alienated and lost. The Congress party did not give adequate representation to the masses in the Pradesh Committee. In the choice of candidates during the first general election, the Bahujan Samaj was relegated to the background. There was a fear that Christians and Brahmins will dominate the Hindu masses. Christians and Brahmans were perceived to be Pro-Portuguese. It was perceived that Maharashtra was the protector of Hindu religion and culture. The attraction to the neighbouring state was also because of social reformers, social reforms, economic reforms, land reforms and egalitarian measures which were enunciated in Maharashtra. Though the Hindu Bahujan Samaj could not speak in proper Marathi and could not read it satisfactorily, still they perceived that Marathi was their cultural language. *"The Goan Hindus asserted that the Goan identity was the pre-Portuguese identity which was no different from larger Indian Identity."* (Arun Sinha: Goa-lndica: pp.15)

The Congress leaders in Maharashtra who were prying on the gifted land of Goa were successful in wooing Dayanand Bandodkar and exploiting the hidden fears of the Goan Bahujan Samaj. For the masses, Bandodkar, fondly known as "Bhau", was a charismatic leader in whom they could identify and trust. Added to this, religious and caste prejudices were at peak. Merger with Maharashtra was directly linked to nationalism and patriotism and this giant state provided the moral and material support to the cause of merger. P. K. Atre roared *"Map of Maharashtra will not be complete unless Goa is merged in it. It is natural that a baby is restored to its mother. Goa is Maharashtra's pet child."*

Despite this, Goans and the Bahujan Samaj were lucky. We are all reaping the political, administrative, cultural and economic benefits of statehood. Today, every Goan understands that all communities in Goa would have lost with merger.

Victory For Identity

January 19, 1967 was the day of counting. January 16, 1967 was the day when Goans sealed their fate and asserted their right for a separate identity. This should be the day of introspection for all Goans. Let us consolidate the gains of our separate identity. Controversies are neither few nor new to Goa. The language controversy is settled and dead in theory. Konkani is recognised by Sahitya Academi and has the pride of place in the Eighth Schedule of the Indian Constitution. However, after every Marathi 'sahitya sammelan', it gets revived and refuelled. The same thing is seen in the case of caste and community tensions immediately before and after every election to the legislative assembly or local self- governing bodies. Politicians with vested interests, communal leaders, fanatics and pressmen who have less to do with journalism thrive on such controversies and conflicts.

What is Goan identity (Asmitai)? To my mind, identity can be perceived, it cannot be defined. "Asmitai" means the red soil of Goa. "Asmitai' mean the greenery spread over the four corners of this land. "Asmitai" means the companionship of the sea, the rivers, the streams, the rivulets and the flowing waters. "Asmitai" is seen in the lifestyle of the people inhabiting this land. "Asmitai" means our food style, our music, our songs, our stories, our poetry, our dance, our drama, our folklore and our polyculture. "Asmitai" means the language on our lips which is our true face (not a mask!), the language which has stood with us since time immemorial despite the onslaught of colonial Portuguese and the same being humiliated and disowned by few locals. "Asmitai" means the love and concern for the land. "Asmitai" is the tract of self-respect that we find in every Goan. "Asmital" is the festive spirit in every Goan. "Asmital" is the recognition of the rights and individuality of women and the stark reality that Goa is safe for women at all times. "Asmitai" is seen in our natural and warm hospitality. Goans are trustworthy and assist others without expectations. This trait puzzles Indians from other states. Our "Asmitai" is seen in our God-fearing, religious, pious and peace-loving nature. Goans are Deshbhakts and patriots. However, they have not mastered the art of digging cricket-pitches during Indo- Pakistan matches to prove their loyalty to Bharat.

The threat to identity comes from politicians and from communal elements. These elements beat the drums of language to divide communities. They dig history and raise the fear of "Inquisition". They continue to link some communities to Portuguese, knowing fully well that facts are different They take shelter under the treatise of the Father of Goan freedom struggle, Tristao Braganza Cunha, entitled "Denationalization of Goans ". These are all attempts to "Degoanise Goans". The truth is that the freedom fighters from the Christian community outnumber those from the majority comunity in percentage terms, in relation to the total population of the two communities.

Goa and Goans have a separate identity. There is something in Goan culture and lifestyle which lures any outsider to fall in love with the place and the people. In addition to our language, Konkani, there are many attributes which bind all Goans irrespective of religion and caste and gives them the sense of belonging to the soil. This Heaven on Earth is an emotional land for Goans all over the world. Opinion poll gave us the opportunity to assert our identity. Let us consolidate and strengthen this "Asmitai" for which the people struggled and guard it at all costs from greedy political and communal elements parading under the guise of patriotism and language. Goa is neither the Rome of the East, nor the Kashi of the South. Goa is "neighbour's envy, owner's pride.

Let Opinion Poll not be a Tomb of Asmitai

Opinion Poll, 1967, the event that shaped Goa's destiny was actually spine-chilling borderline arithmetic which kept the tiny region Goa separate to graduate into an independent State in 1987. The final outcome could have gone anyway if the opinion poll was fought and perceived only on language. It would therefore not be correct to reduce the results of opinion poll as a linguistic victory. The Goan community is a unique cultural group rooted to the soil, sharing common lifestyle irrespective of religion. It was the triumph of this human geography of the petite land which can boast of being a brand known worldwide for being a community manifested in secular traditions, liberal mind-set, unique cuisine, festive spirit, zest for life and a tolerant outlook. Against the backdrop of Goa's demographic disadvantage on account of the relative disability of numbers it was imperative for Goa to be maintained as a separate democratic unit.

The debate on whether Goa could preserve the uniqueness of the Goan community and guard its identity (*Asmitai*) may not end with a clear affirmative answer. But definitely, Goa and Goans had access to all the democratic tools. Failures to make the best of opportunities are discernible. At the same time, the balance sheet of 57 years also record gains of opinion poll though accompanied by damages. Goa's merger with any neighbouring State would have been a wash out of Brand Goa and the pride of the macro community.

On Goa's way forward, migration and immigration are turning out to be threats and challenges. Both these are not new as Goans have the tradition of migration from early times. This microscopic minority has excelled in art, architecture, music, philosophy; sports etc. at international levels and have strong presence overseas. Despite migration what differentiates Goans is the sense of belonging and love for the land. Migration continues to be a means to escape from poverty and for a better quality of life. There is no conflict between migration and attachment to the soil. The reasons for immigration into Goa are also the same. Goa is perceived as the land of opportunities by the poor and unemployed from neighbouring states. The vacuum created by migration is occupied through immigration. In the years to come, these less privileged sections of immigrants could be those who preserve the language and culture. I would submit that those who immigrate to satisfy their basic needs would serve Goa in future as opposed to those who storm Goa for speculative investments in land and real estate or motivated by Goa as a retreat destination.

The new saplings of communal hate and discord planted and nursed by fanatical groups and irrigated by political elements is the major threat to Goa's identity. These regressive forces attack Goa's diversity as appeasement of minorities. There are attempts to project Christians as anti-development because of projected worry that development results in influx of Hindus. Gullible Hindus fall easy prey to such propaganda little knowing the loss to Goans as a whole. The fundamentalist tuned elements are competing to match "every Cross on the street with a Tulsi Vrundavan and every chapel with a temple" and both these forces would join together to deny even a burial place to Muslims!

During the days of the Opinion Poll agitation, the forces who espoused merger would describe Goan Christians as pro-Portuguese and today the Hindutva political brigade is making similar claims and dumps those who oppose coal and river nationalization as anti-national and unpatriotic. It is this positioning and implant of social venom that poses irreversible damage to Goa, Goemkar and Goemkarponn.

Finally, *"Asmitai"* is Goa's poly-culture. To live in harmony with nature and people respecting the freedom and privacy of individual comes naturally to a Niz Goenkar.

The way forward is to ensure that development and politics which works to the detriment of the above is dis-allowed as it is an anti-thesis of the struggle of the Opinion Poll. Goa is still known as a pious, peaceful and tolerant land. Goans are respected and known for their respect to diversity and individual freedom. The ugly clouds of pollution, social disharmony, drugs, prostitution and rabid nationalism are hovering over this land. They should not be allowed to crystallize into rain on the soil of Goa. Otherwise, 16th January would be the date to light candles on the tomb of *"Asmitai."*

Futureless or Futuristic Agriculture!

Let me begin with four perceptions about agriculture in Goa which are also the stumbling blocks for the renaissance of this sector to ensure sustainable growth of rural areas.

1) The agricultural sector in Goa is dead and there is no scope for revival even through a transplant surgery. This dominant view gathers support from the fact that only around 16% of Goa's work force is engaged in agriculture sector and the same is registering continuous decline. Further, the contribution of agriculture to the State Domestic Product is now a meagerly 7%. The productivity of all crops has declined with marginal exception of cashew, arecanut and coconut. With land under cultivation declining and the cultivable land area kept fallow increasing, the projected vision is of decaying agriculture as a source of livelihood, employment and income.

2) There is no future for youth tied to agriculture; hence the deliberate and conscious movement is seen to industry and service sectors.

3) Industry and service sectors are attractive economic activities; agriculture is repulsive for Generation Next. This is because the traditional picture of agriculture using bullock power and labour-intensive farming stands ingrained.

4) Agriculture is good as a hobby for the individual and for the corporate as Corporate Social Responsibility; stand alone it's not viable and rewarding.

Contrast this with the market reality to draw implications for agriculture on commercial lines. Goa is totally dependent on neighbouring states for fruits, vegetables, flowers and spices. This indicates the market potential for such crops. In specific crops such as cashew, coconut and arecanut where organized marketing chains are available the business model is presently a success story in Goa. There is a formal marketing structure in respect of fisheries and animal husbandry such as dairy and poultry. This is a pointer for the need of such farmer-trader-consumer chains for other crops. Agriculture, horticulture and allied activity could run complementary and blend well with the tourism industry. This suggests that the tourism-agriculture linkage will prove mutually beneficial. The state has the gift of natural resource with a reasonable irrigation network and traditional water sources in the hinterland talukas of Pernem, Sattari, Ponda, Sanguem and Canacona. Cultivable land is available but the land kept fallow is increasing every year. Organic farming, local varieties of pulses (like 'alsando'), medicinal crops could also form a part of commercial agriculture in Goa. The farms need to be reformed into agricultural firms by setting up of agricultural estates following the model of industrial estates to facilitate agro-based entrepreneurship. Contract farming has to be explored so that cultivable lands are exploited.

Agriculture undoubtedly suffers from the image sickness being associated as an occupation for unskilled workers and dropouts from the formal educational system. Image and glamour comes through academic recognitions. Diploma courses after higher secondary education and certificate courses for those who cannot complete high school education would improve the image graph of those who pursue agriculture. Agriculture Training Institutes (ATI) on the lines of Industrial Training Institutes (ITI) can take this thought further. Two colleges for pursuing a graduate programme in agriculture cum management would answer the requirements of the aspirational learner segment. A branch of agricultural engineering at Goa Engineering College should evolve. All this could be brought under the umbrella of an Agricultural University & Extension Education. Such a network would restore the image and build the confidence of the aspirants. Without a big push to education, innovative approaches including use of advanced machinery in agriculture may be a far cry.

Agriculture department has a laundry list of schemes and incentive cum subsidy packages. Still, the overall climate does not provide any assurance of revival. Probably, we have not succeeded to locate what is exactly needed. The pitifully small thrust is not propelling the agricultural vehicle into an acceptable proposition for growth of rural areas and occupations. The mining boom had eclipsed agriculture in the rural areas, specifically the mining belt. The larger gamut of agriculture, horticulture, floriculture and agri-eco tourism should be looked at very seriously to answer the vacuum of gainful opportunities.

Section 2.

Goa in Transition

> *This section familiarizes the quest of Goa from being a Union territory to become an autonomous state in comparison with other states, addressing the rationales prompting its journey. The writer sketches the emotional attachment of Goans who dissented against the merger, to save their distinct identity and the confidence of the same Goans who re-elected MGP, (who espoused merger) after the Opinion Poll.*
>
> *Additionally, the author makes the reader aware about the development trap and the vulnerability of small states in the absence of an active civil society and vigilant institutions.*

Small States, Better Governance

Starting with 16 states in 1971, India today is a union of 28 states with the creation of Chhattisgarh, Jharkhand and Uttarakhand in the year 2000 and Telangana in 2014. We have 8 Union Teritories after Ladakh was delineated from Jammu & Kashmir (2019). Dadara & Nagar Haveli and Daman & Diu got designated as a single union teritory (2020). With the development experience of the new states vis-à-vis the stagnation these regions faced when they were part of the linguistic-based larger group of states, many neglected regions rightly feel that they need their own governments if the regions and people have to thrive.

Though earlier, the states were re-organised on linguistic basis, the big states have proved to be unwieldy in terms of governance. Politicians in power are also found wanting in working beyond their elected constituencies. The success stories of development, enrichment and empowerment of the limited pockets in the big states, many times at the cost of the resources of the neglected regions in the state is the cause of imergence of small states. The economic backwardness due to neglect coupled with cultural homogeneity of such regions is fomenting genuine demands for new states to be carved from existing big states.

Reorganise for balance

Gorkhas in West Bengal are demanding Gorkhaland, the Bodo tribe demand Bodoland separate from Assam, Bundelkhand and Harit Pradesh are being claimed as separate states from Uttar Pradesh. The long standing cry for Telengana from Andhra Pradesh has become a reality. Despite constitutional guarantees to Vidarbha and Saurashtra, these regions in Maharashtra and Gujarat respectively remain uncared for by successive governments.

Apart from these demands, maybe India should go for a new re-organisation of States. At present, U.P., Maharashtra, West Bengal, A.P. are bigger than France or Great Britain. Census wise, U.P. has overtaken Russia or Pakistan. The percentage of population below the poverty line in Maharashtra is higher than the national average. Probably, if you eject 'Amchi Mumbai', Maharashtra would be an underdeveloped state. With narrow parochialism of the Shiv Sena, the competition between this Sena and the Raj Thackeray Maharashtra Navnirman Sena for the regional chauvinism crown and the violence with Tamil, Kannada, Malayalam and Hindi speaking immigrants is a stumbling block for talent to land in Mumbai. Added to this is the overcrowded infrastructure and deteriorating quality of life. Working out a policy for optimum sized States rather than a response to burning of buses, agitations and destruction of public property would facilitate the development of all the regions.

The great India bazaar

A summing up of India could be drawn from the words of the American humourist, Mark Twain: *"This is India! The land of dreams and romance, of fabulous wealth and fabulous poverty, of splendour and rags, of palaces and hovels, of famine and pestilence, of genie and giants and Aladdin lamps, of tigers and elephants, the cobra and the jungle, the country of a hundred nations and a hundred tongues, of a thousand religions and two million gods, cradle of the human race, birth place of human speech, mother of history, grandmother of legend, great grandmother of tradition, whose yesterday's bear date with the mouldering antiquities of the rest of the nations the one sole country under the sun that is endowed with an imperishable interest for alien persons, four-lettered and ignorant, wise and fool, rich and poor, bond and free, the one land all men desire to see, and having seen once, by even a glimpse, would not give that glimpse for all the shows of all the rest of the globe combined."*

This picture of India is not a weakness. It is strength. In economic terms, India is a very big, diverse and great Bazaar. Regional autonomy is required for development of all regions mainly due to the size and diversity. It is against this background that we should evaluate the demand for smaller states.

Empirical studies have shown that regions which were parts of big states had high rates of economic growth once they were formed into separate states. This was true of Haryana after delinking from Punjab. The carving of Chhattisgarh and Jharkhand made the desired difference to the economic development of these two otherwise neglected regions. The other benefits are in terms of improvement in quality of administration, accessibility to citizens and grassroots representation in democratic institutions.

Small is politics but......

Small is beautiful but small is also politics. Small states are vulnerable to be taken over by closed groups or lobbies. This can defeat the purpose of establishing small states and the benefits associated with it mainly for the neglected regions and people. A few greedy politicians in collusion with mining and real estate lobbies can derail empowerment of the poor in the otherwise neglected regions. This minority group can have a pervasive hold on all democratic institutions starting with the local governing bodies. The only corrective for this is active civil society and vigilant institutions. Side by side with regional autonomy, people should eschew narrow regional jingoism which may erode the Indian republic.

Small states are not a threat to a strong nation. Let us also understand that a strong nation does not exist, it has to be created. Regional aspirations in a diverse nation should be respected. But, we should not gloat in matters such as the 'Telugu or Tamil' pride. The tone and body language in which we shout *"Maharashtra mazza ani mi Maharashtracha"* exhibiting arrogance towards people from other States is like winning the battle for the State and losing the war for the nation. The RSS oft repeated *"Akhandh Bharat"* and *"Hindu Rashtra"* keeps an otherwise rich national human resource away from building the republic. In the recent years, the Congress could throw largely pygmies as leaders at the national and state levels. The appeal of the cudgel of secularism that this party claims to hold is brutally washed in the downpour of corruption at all levels. Somehow, we have devalued secularism linking it as beneficial to minorities, not understanding that secularism is bonded to democracy, equality and justice. It is an inseparable tenet of civilised governance and public administration equally important for the majority community. Secularism is in fact humanism.

To conclude, I would say that India should go for a reorganisation of states to ensure development of all regions and the belts which have remained backward even after 75 years of independence. The risk if any does not lie in small states. It lies in the growing feeling that politics is the *"Note Chapne ki Machine."*

Too much Government, Declining Governance

Statistically, Goa stands as one of the best developed states in the country. Apart from being a brand by itself due to the natural gifts and the proverbial social harmony, Goa stands very high on per capita income index. The same is true of the human development indicators in terms of access to basic needs, primary education, health, public utilities and women empowerment.

Importing the famous quote of the former Business Professor Aaron Levenstein, "Statistics are like a bikini, what they reveal is interesting, but what they hide is vital", I would say that Goa has been a victim of too much government and declining standards of governance over the years. Goa still looks beautiful because it is small. Goa bags front ranks mainly being petite. However, small gets easily infected with politics of all sorts. It is the politics of religion, caste and language superimposed with the partisan and greedy politics in government that has derailed governance. Goa, as described by Kakasaheb Kalelkar as the 'land of the virtuous and pious' is today internationally known for drug traffic, sex crimes and pedophilia. The collapse of governance is seen in terms of environmental pollution, menace of solid waste and deteriorating law and order. The fact that Goa is not rated as a friendly investment destination (except by land sharks and polluting enterprises) also speaks of weak governance and non-visionary leadership. The scarcity of the land resource of Goa sets limitations on its use and exploitation. At the same time, we keep this land resource idle, fallow and unutilized as if the resource is in plenty. This is seen in respect of land held by Comunidades, land transferred to tenants under the Agricultural Tenancy Act and land acquired by the government for industrial estates, public purpose and for private companies.

Public delivery mechanisms

Despite a highly bloated 1:27 bureaucrats to citizen ratio, where the huge chunk of government revenue is eaten up by salary and pension payments, the public delivery mechanisms can hardly be said to be quick, responsive, accountable and transparent. The common citizen and self-employed, expect small things from the government. They are in the nature of licenses, approvals, "sanads", mutations, occupancy certificates, access to public utilities (water, power) and business related permits and clearances. All these are infested with delays and under-hand payments. Though, a Public Services Guarantee Act has been enacted, the implementation is tardy. People will perceive that Goa is well-governed only when the delivery of public services is time-bound and corruption-free.

The new challenges before the law and order machinery i.e. the police department is cyber crimes, gender related offences and 'crimes without victims'. At the same time, use and absorption of better technology in crime detection and prevention is an opportunity. The stinking corruption in the police wing, custodial violence, police theft and open political interference is responsible for the public image of the police as being criminal-friendly.

Transparent, clean and professional

No state in the country has played political football with the State Information Commission and the State Lokayukta machinery as much as the BJP government in Goa. SIC is practically defunct from the day the BJP took over the reins of governance in 2012 and the former Chief Minister Manohar Parrikar worked to make it an over-advertised failure. The same Chief Minister took high moral ground amending the Goa Lokayukta Act to ensure that the incumbent to the post as per the amended provision is hard to get. Further, the Chief Minister made use of the State Vigilance Department to initiate proceedings against political rivals with none being brought to any logical conclusion. Inquiries are hanging for over five years against suspended police officers involved in drug trade. The same holds true in respect of proceedings against bureaucrats caught accepting bribes. Good governance demands that these statutory autonomous institutions function without a break and the Vigilance Department functions under the supervision and control of the Lokayukta. A government which has put both key institutions meant to monitor clean and transparent governance in cold storage goes to indicate that transparency and corruption free governance is not recognized as the priority by the government.

Decentralisation of power is an accepted principle of good and participative governance. No ruling government in Goa is prepared to effectively share power with Panchayats and urban bodies. The absence of the State Finance Commission (SFC) to earmark resources for local bodies and evolve criteria for devolution of powers has made grass-root democratic institutions vulnerable to the whims of the ruling political party. It would not be wrong to say that the Zilla Panchayats exist only as ornaments with almost no functions to perform. Of late, it is learnt that the SFC has submitted the report to the government.

Government Corporations are kept outside legislative scrutiny. At the same time they are packed not just with rank politicians but pure party- men. Appointment of professionals is treated as impurity. If properly investigated, the Goa State Infrastructure Development Corporation would emerge as the biggest scam in the State. Mere E-tendering does not bring down corruption as the GSIDC offers rip-off rates which would not stand the tests for public works.

Fiscal discipline & land governance

Three most critical issues for Goa Tomorrow in the domain of governance would be fiscal discipline, optimum utilization of scarce land resource and time-bound delivery of public services. The government needs to step up its public revenue through improved tax administration and compliance as revenue deficits are expected. If a clear policy of Public-Private Partnership is put in place, private resources can be augmented for Education, Infrastructure and Townships adjoining the present five major towns-----Margao, Panaji, Vasco, Mapusa and Ponda.

The state will find it difficult to maintain the tempo of economic growth unless lands lying idle with the State Industrial Development Corporation, tenants, Comunidade and with other government departments are effectively harnessed. A model will have to be worked out to guarantee that any further land acquisition provides long-term benefits to the dispossessed.

Amchem Goem:
The Sweet and Sad Chapters

Harmony in social relations, balance in environment, a culture of acceptance and tolerance, poise in personal life and synchronisation in every aspect of human endeavour is the major component of the sweet chapter of Goan community life. The later part of the first fifty years of liberated Goa has witnessed attacks on this harmony. The sourness has set in with everybody making inroads into this proverbial harmony. Goa is a small cosmopolitan State and a presence in Goa, means a presence in one State of India. This is the approach of political parties, outfits dishing religious, spiritual and 'patriotic' products; all shades of Ram or Vanar Sena; all shadows of Durga Vahini and Bajrang Dal of all colours have gradually injected doses of hatred and false notions of patriotism and nationalism to divide communities. Goa is vulnerable to this because it is considered to be a good ground for testing by all organisations and NGOs. All are working for a share in Goa. As we move beyond fifty, the threat of the secular, progressive and seekers of harmony being reduced to minority looms large. Norman Dantas described our land as a place where "disagreements are dissolved with jest." We are losing or might have already lost this great tradition.

Although liberated in 1961 from the Portuguese, the first 25 years has witnessed the struggle for a different liberation. Hence, Goans lost valuable years of qualitative and positive growth asserting their identity to soil, culture and language. In the Opinion Poll, 44.5% chose merger with Maharashtra, though finally Goa retained its separate identity. The native language was looked down upon by majority of Hindus and elite Catholics. The first popular government established primary schools in Marathi medium throughout Goa, thereby sending the signal that Konkani cannot be accorded the status of a language. The victory of anti-merger forces, the official status to Konkani, recognition by Sahitya Academy and the grant of statehood are all sweet events. All these controversies now remain settled. The sad chapter is that, many are still hesitant to accept and embrace Konkani as the language identity of all Goans. That's why even in 2011, we come together under the banner of "Bharatiya Sanskruti Manch" and not "Konkani Sanskruti Manch" because we are still unsure of the unity of Goans to accept that only Konkani is the mother-tongue of Goans worldwide. The communal forces are gleefully having a jolly good ride by planting rodents in the secular Konkani force.

You will not see such a contradiction in any other state of India! Mother-tongue anywhere else unites the community. In Goa, it still continues to divide. The roots of this lie in the seeds sown during the days of the Opinion Poll, the primary education policy of the Maharashtrawadi Gomantak Party which ruled Goa in the formative years and the hunger for political gains out of language and communal divide.

The sweetest thing about Goa is its undemanding and non-invasive culture and about Goans is their friendly lifestyle. Goans have a natural gift of saying enough to need and greed. The saddest thing is these aspects are misrepresented and this harms the true picture of a God-fearing, peace-loving and trustworthy community. Tourism promoters project Goa as a "Mouj-Masti ka Pradesh", Goan cuisine as Portuguese and Goans as descendants of Portuguese. The rest of India looks at Goa as a location where drinking is a way of life and that Goans are people out to have good time. **We market Goa not as it actually is, but as tourists and other Indians want to see. For sustainable and quality tourism, this vulgarity should be brought to a full stop.**

Goa's march to social and economic equity deserves mention. The land to the tiller legislation, The Mundkar Act and the Bahujan Samaj taking control of local self-governing institutions are the soothing winds of change and development. The gloomy side is lands kept fallow, alienation of lands to non-locals and the representatives of OBC, SC/ST using their less privileged brethren as doormats to enter the world of greed. They use the name of the oppressed but once in power and position, they just do not represent their community. The tragedy of Goa is total lack of pure social leadership and progressive thinkers across communities. As opposed to this, the neighbouring States are fortunate to have it in abundance.

The saddest of all is Goans being ridiculed by the outside world due to distasteful and disgraceful politics and politicians. We have reduced politics to gaming and gambling. Our state legislature resembles an on-shore casino. Even otherwise, all 'successful' politicians are frequent customers at casinos and they have also converted the Secretariat into a venue for dealing, brokerage and commissions. And Goans aggressively and jubilantly work as cheerleaders for these jokers and prove to the world that Goa is free for all and Goans are clowns!

Goa Needs a Growth Story

Goa falls in the category of the most developed States of the Indian Union with the highest per capita income. If the Human Development Index (HDI) is construed in terms of access to education, health, public goods such as roads, power, water, social infrastructure and financial products, Goa is indeed fortunate. Whether scams, corruption and loot lubricated this development or whether in their absence the visible development would have been still better is another debate which I would refrain from at this stage. Despite a highly educated and literate population and an almost zero population growth, Goa faces a serious problem of unemployment. Looking at the immigration of workforce into Goa, it looks like there is also the issue of unemployableness and disagreeableness of locals to certain occupations.

Goa needs a sustainable growth model rather than a rejection of growth. Growth could increase inequalities in the initial stages is well established by economists. But, with a mix of economic decentralisation, social sector spending and fiscal consolidation that growth and equity go together is also demonstrated by growth models. I also stand by the hypothesis that a slump in growth also increases inequalities by aggravating poverty on the one hand and reducing access to goods and opportunities on account of reduced purchasing power. Everybody talks of sustainable development without specifics. This is a rifle in our armoury to shoot down growth initiatives. At the most, we are vocal on what is not sustainable growth rather than putting the logistics and essentials of growth models considering the natural, land, human resources and identity concerns of the State.

Looking at the past one decade of Goa's growth, it is amply evident that growth is different from development. The absence of growth strategy is writ large looking at the uncontrolled progression of mining industry and the related logistics. More than the anti-mining lobby, it is the beneficiaries of the mining industry including the politicians, who stand vicariously responsible for the current stalemate. Growth of industrial estates has not been accompanied by a sound base for industrial growth due to the absence of a composite strategy. It was a total 'laissez-faire' approach anybody can open any shop anywhere, anyhow and anytime. The approach to growth of tourism and hospitality industry was also no different.

The two models of growth which are hotly discussed today are those that emanate from the stories of Gujarat and Bihar. Both the States are dissimilar in terms of natural and human resources but the common thread is the optimism and the pride for the region-State generated by the respective political and bureaucratic machinery. Both the growth models are focussed to free economic space for private initiative and enterprise with the government creating enabling environment. Both models have increased the expectation levels through bureaucratic empowerment. Mr. Nitish Kumar has been successful to change the agenda of the politics of Bihar which was a dump of bribery, extortion, abduction and caste. So to say, these were the economic activities of Bihar and the state was in a poverty trap with income declining every year. Today, Bihar speaks a story for other states to emulate. The Gujarat model of growth has harnessed the tradition and culture of private entrepreneurship to ensure a trickle-down effect. There is criticism that the strategy is capital-intensive and discriminatory. The India Human Development Report (2011) underscores that the high growth rates achieved by the state of Gujarat over the years has not percolated to the marginalised sections of the society. These are areas on which public expenditure could be pumped through specific schemes but should in no way belittle the growth in terms of the Gross State Domestic Product.

There are sound lessons for Goa worth importing. Goa in the recent past and present is extravagantly projecting negativism. Gujarat injected a solid dose of a positive outlook by wooing investment pushed out by other states. Both Gujarat and Bihar has improved on the efficiency of public expenditure in terms of cost and time. There is an attempt towards fiscal consolidation through stepping up of public revenue and a focus on creating opportunities for private expenditure. What is more notable is the tuning of public administration to make it responsive and responsible to the call of business and investment. The political executive in this states expects the bureaucracy to achieve the growth objectives.

Mere talks of identity without a push to growth and employment will not help Goa and its people. The government has to hoist a growth model for the state and sow the seeds of sustainable development with specific and clear policies and programmes. Regulations such as buffer zones, coastal regulation zones, and green zones should not be considered as "untouchable" locations for development. These locations need to be preserved in the interests of business, people and their occupations. They would remain preserved and protected only if these locations are utilised and exploited productively for people. Preservation is for sustained development and not to keep the resources in a state of idleness. By development, I also do not mean merely excavation, extraction and road infrastructure. However, the curtain of negativism would prove negative for Goa's 'Asmitai' and environment.

Goa: Demography Versus Development

Goa is India's smallest state in terms of land area. It is also a tiny state in terms of population. It is India's richest state in terms of per capita income. It is ranked on top, judged on the Human Development Index. The Brand Goa signifies natural beauty, tolerance, harmony and zest for life. From a population of 5.90 lakh in 1961, it has touched 15.75 lakh in 2023. Though Goan's are unkind to the immigrants and hold the inflow of unskilled and semi-skilled with disdain and contempt, it has been the Goan tradition to migrate particularly overseas for employment. Goans justify this migration due to lack of resourceful and gainful opportunities at home. However, immigration into Goa for the same reasons from the neighbouring states is perceived as threat. The immigrants are painted as polluting agents and held responsible for dirt, stench, thefts and crime. Today, the educated and skilled youth of Goa are forced to migrate as Goa is considered as a land of limited opportunities. The absence or deficiency of infrastructure and mechanical opposition to development is also putting a compulsory burden on talent, investors and entrepreneurs to spend their productive years beyond the Goan borders.

A Futureless Goa!

The sweetest songs of Goa continue to be of past thoughts. Ringing in the new develops ulcers in elderly locals and vocal section of global Goans. Goans stay contented as long as they can peacefully perform their non-productive rituals in the temple and the church. Under the garb of identity and environment, opposition to any type of development has gripped Goa. Though, in certain projects dissent and hostility is justified, it should not happen that Goa is condemned to be a retreat house to partake chicken 'cafreal' and fish 'reshado' in between pegs of scotch and 'feni'. *The threat that development brings immigration and thus disturbs demography should not make negativism as the banner head-line to describe the state. Development cannot be the victim of demography as a futureless Goa will not retain its youth on the soil.* At the same time, demography should not be the inevitable price of development putting Goa out of control of locals at a shocking speed.

Let me put it straight. What does Goa expect in terms of development and opportunities? Let me answer it directly. Looking at the opposition from NGOs, the Council for Social Justice & Peace (CSJP) and the village-groups with strong nexus to the church, the expectation is probably nothing. It is evident that status quo would keep them satisfied as long as the faithful stay immersed in prayers at the stroke of church bells. Over the last decade, all these groups have opposed everything without exception. At the same time, none has proposed any alternative to answer the challenge of employment, infrastructure and opportunities to realize the hopes and aspirations of Generation Next.

The government had put the issue of Regional Plan in cold storage due to the negativism and the failure to put up concrete alternative by the forces who oppose. The Regional Plan was not notified providing unguided power to the executive. There is opposition to Special Economic Zones, housing projects, garbage plants and real estate projects. Each one of us wants to use two-wheeler and four-wheeler vehicles and yet raise a storm on broadening of roads and highways. We want mobiles without mobile towers. We cannot come to a consensus on providing land for National Institute of Technology (NIT) and Indian Institute of Technology (IIT). The doubling of Vasco-Hospet railway line would also not face a congenial weather. The sickness to oppose has also spread to marina projects.

Propose & dispose

If every development is opposed as anti-Goan, then it is also the responsibility to put in ink what is pro-Goa. If certain locations are not suitable for certain activities then alternative locations need to be proposed. Development is needed for employment. It is only investment in infrastructure and economic activities that can further improve the quality of life. It is growth which provides alternatives and tones the freedom of choices in production, consumption, distribution and exchange.

Ecology and environmental concerns are understandable. Compliance to laws in this regard is expected rather than blanket opposition. The concern that development should benefit the locals in terms of employment and self-employment is logical and reasonable. Demographic changes are taking place in all cities such as Mumbai, Hyderabad, Chennai, Bangalore, and Pune and two-tier towns such as Kolhapur, Ratnagiri and Mangalore. Goa would not remain an exception as it is a concomitant of development.

The clear writing on the wall is that without investment and industry, Goa cannot be a land of opportunities. It is also clear that migration and immigration are inevitable for economic growth and human development. A blanket opposition to development can retain Goa for the joy of the retired and for those Goans and outsiders who consider the state as a family holiday destination. It is for the youth who desire to make Goa as their home and for the immigrants who desire to make a productive contribution for mutual benefit that the land of sun and sand should also be the terra firma of business, industry and education.

Opposition to Projects Will Harm Goa--I

Portuguese Goa was basically and totally an agrarian economy. Though it is generally propagated that Goans were successful with agriculture, horticulture and fisheries as Goans had adopted the art of doing business with nature, this is not something exclusive about only Goa. This is true of the village communities of the earlier times in other parts of the country where the majority sweated for survival and subsistence and the land resource was locked in the hands of miniscule minority. The majority was poor with no access to education, health and consumer goods which ensure a quality lifestyle. As observed in "Fish, Curry and Rice- A Citizen's Report on the State of the Goan Environment (Goa Foundation: 1993)", Portugal was comparatively unindustrialized compared to the other nations of Europe. Secondly, Portugal saw to it that Goa had consumer goods without having to undergo the rigours associated with industries producing such goods. It was bountiful and enchanting nature that made Goa golden. The economic disparity and social inequity was a cruel reality in 'Bhangralem (golden) Goem' where 85% had to struggle for survival. It is the creamy and landed minority who could merrily bathe in the golden waters and streams of Goa and tom-tom Goa as paradise on Earth sipping the proverbial "feni" feasting on 'Chicken Cafreal' and 'Mackerel Reshado' which today are Goa's signature items on the menu cards of the growing hotel industry in the state.

Goa's march to modern economy can be largely accounted due to service sector with trading forming the major component. Trading has been Goa's forte in view of the natural Mormugao port and inland waterways. Immediately prior to liberation of Goa and in the initial period post-1961, it is development of mining and export of ores that fuelled the economy of the state. Further, Goans have been migrating out of Goa through the ages. Consequently, it was the remittances along with mining, shipbuilding and ancillary industries that shaped the quality of life of Goans. Later, the reckless and insatiable greed that gripped the industry, more epecifically mining and real estate, resulted in the adverse impact on lifestyle, health and environment of Goa and Goans.

Migrants in the courtyard

The above phrase is borrowed from Arun Sinha's book "Goa Indica" which aptly reflects the pain and anxiety of Goans. It is natural for migration and immigration to become the concomitant of a trading economy. The migrant population embracing unskilled jobs is to escape the poverty in their native place. This is the chunk of marginal farmers or agricultural labourers who are seasonally employed, hence looking out for subsistence employment in construction projects, industrial estates, ports, farms, plantations or extractive industries at new locations. Some of them could be displaced from their land due to land acquisition for infrastructure projects in their native place. During the agricultural season, these migrants would return to their native locations to fall back on their low yielding agriculture. It is such migrants which Goans refer to as "Ghanti" and hold them responsible for the dirt and filth in the state, though many of these migrants are engaged in waste collection and management. These are productive workers involved in asset creation in Goa. They live in despicable conditions, unloved and uncared despite having land and dwelling at their native place.

Another category of migrants are those who find opportunities in small business such as retail, wholesale merchandise and in service sector involving para-engineering skills. These migrants find such opportunities in prime cities and two-tier towns. It is this category that shows tendency of settling down at the new location and become permanent residents with their children learning in schools and becoming part of the local community. With Goans taking the route of vertical mobility in employment, professions and occupations, it is the migrants who fill the vacuum as toddy tappers, bakers, housemaids, cooks, waiters, dishwashers, grocery merchants, fruit and vegetable vendors and security personnel. The economy and regular life would be paralyzed if these human resources are sacked being migrants.

It is an open secret that Goan entrepreneurs in mining, fisheries, real estate, exports and hotels prefer migrant labour with a mix of locals. This should not happen at the cost of local employment is to be accepted without debate. Goa is also a manpower exporter and Goans leave the shores for more remunerative jobs and opportunities in other parts of the country and the world.

If Goa has lost or continues to lose it is largely due to the investors and speculators in property and real estate. This lobby continues to be residents of metro cities putting land and housing outside the reach of not only the locals but a common man who has migrated to Goa to make it as his home. The onslaught on the agricultural land of Goa also comes from this outside capital that makes offers which locals cannot refuse. It is in this area where the intervention of the government and the state legislature is required to arrest speculation and alienation of scarce land resource.

Document for future

Development will never be a smooth process. It will create economic imbalances, demographic changes and disturb the old social power order. Traditional culture, however pure and serene the Goans may feel, it cannot stay immune to development. The traditional elements of Goan life would come under attack as the case with all the communities in the rest of the country and the world. The expectation and aspiration of the new generation of Goans is change keeping the cultural identity of Goa as reflected in social harmony, tolerance and diversity as non-negotiable. Gen-Next wants Goa to be a land of opportunities without irreparable damage to environment.

Opposition to Projects Will Harm Goa-II

Today, the casino indusrty is taking charge of Goa's economy and politics to the extent that the politicians have converted state politics into a gambling den by playing the game of defections. The fever of opposition to projects is to some extent justifiable. Post-1990, the political and business leadership has failed Goa and the nexus has worked to the detriment of local interests. Mining has been the mainstay of the Goan economy which accelerated the careers and made lives of families since liberation. It was the recklessness coupled with the merger of political leadership with mining lobby that derailed environment, ecology, agriculture and horticulture. Establishment of industrial estates was needed for development of small and medium enterprises. However, a sell out to power guzzling and polluting units employing largely contract migrant labour made people question expansion of existing and setting up of new industrial estates. Lack of transparency and rampant corruption resulted in cornering of industrial plots by public officers and politicians. Tourism is undeniably the potent sector for Goa provided we make an ideal integration with hinterlands and exploit the opportunity for handicrafts, art and culture, entertainment, events and conventions, and agro-processing industry. The economic, social and political decay of the entire beach belt in North Goa ring the bells sounding the funeral procession of the tourism industry being buried in the cemetery of drugs, casinos and prostitution. The threat perception of the land getting alienated from the hands of locals and from agriculture is an imminent reality which is at the root of the negativism pervading in Goa. As a result, any attempt of the government to acquire land or put the same in the hands of business group is resented.

Trade, Finance & Tourism

Having said the above let me underscore that the state cannot afford to stay in pessimistic and gloomy mode. Hence, it is necessary to identify areas and projects which offer the least costs in terms of land, environment and migrants. The same should provide maximum benefits in terms of employment and growth opportunities for youth and entrepreneurs. As compared to other states, Goa is not fortunate to get an intelligent, honest, risk-taking and hardworking political and business leaders.

A reading of early history, more specifically the writings of Shenoi Goembab (Samagra Shenoi Goembab: Konkani Academy: Vol- 2) clearly reveal that from the very early times, Goa has been a centre of trade and commerce. Hence, naturally it has been cosmopolitan being the land frequented by people of different religions, race and colour. Migration is not a recent phenomenon in the state. It is also wrong to presume that Goa has been a land of milk and honey during the colonial rule. On *"The Rice Problem"*, T. B. Cunha states "The quantity produced by each cultivator is generally hardly enough for his own domestic consumption". He provides an account of how emigration of Goans to Africa and mostly in towns in India and more conspicuous in Bombay for *"collar & tie"* proletariat of small office-clerks was due to poor economic conditions and agricultural ruin. If earlier, emigration was due to poverty and search for bread, today it is mainly due to absence of opportunities and growing aspirations.

A government which looks at development as construction of three bridges over the River Mandovi, two bridges over River Sal, two Airports, free train services to Tirupati, Valankanni and Ayodhya, statues of Emperors and rebuilding of temples is one which has run out of ideas. It is such unproductive and wasteful government expenditure that comes in the way of building public confidence and congenial attitude to development projects.

Trade is and has been Goa's strength largely due to a natural harbour. Goans are also naturally inclined to multiple language skills. The 450 years of Portuguese rule should have made the language intelligible to the local population but we did not create any space for the same. Negative patriotism came in the way of converting this international link language as an asset for future of our youth.

Goa should emerge as the key centre for financial services which includes banking and insurance. Trading and E-commerce are suitable and desirable areas. To strengthen the tourism sector, Goa needs to be developed for conventions, events, marinas, home-stay and as a second home for high spending tourists. Working from home could be harnessed into working from Goa. Considering the environment and land resource in the state, the priority in terms of industrialization should be medium engineering units, pharmaceuticals, health, electronics and information technology. This could happen only if there is a highly incentivized climate in terms of tax holidays and special economic zones coupled with efficient public administration and services.

Without industrialization there cannot be opportunities is the bottom-line to be accepted. We speak of opportunities for agriculture, horticulture and floriculture. This is a possibility if and only when these are converted into a modern industry. If the government raises the infrastructure, Goa could be a hub for performing arts, visual arts and films. A free flow of investment should be encouraged in the field of speciality education and knowledge industry. It is a sin to starve this sector for land. At the same time, extravagance and land storage for future should be disallowed. Goa could be made the location for all types of educational, training and research institutions.

Language & Culture

Any growing economy and society tends to be multilingual. This cannot be perceived to be threat to the local language. If we respect multilingualism, there will be less risk to Konkani. Economic interests in a globalised world are better served by international and national languages. Earlier, Konkani stagnated due to persecution during four centuries of Portuguese rule. After liberation, not a single school in Konkani was opened by the Goa government for over thirty years. The landlords considered it as the language of servants. The Bahujan Samaj regarded it as the language of their exploiters (Saraswats). A section of Goans loved to flirt with it as a dialect. The present environment for Konkani is conducive than ever before if we do not lock horns on script. A script should not divide Goans. Today's age of Information and Communications Technology (ICT) opens multiple possibilities if we digest that Konkani in all the scripts is the language of the Konkan belt.

Further, a society which considers growth as a right has to also accept that culture cannot remain static with growth. Development facilitates movement towards a progressive culture weeding out the discriminatory and regressive chaff of the past. Technology makes old cultural styles redundant and facilitates fusion of cultures.

The Threat of Negative Activism

Apart from the challenges to culture, identity and language of Goa, the economic threat looms equally large since this small friendly territory is perceived as an investor-enemy destination. The two critical reasons for the investor fatigue are the infrastructure bottlenecks and the endless bureaucratic red tape. There are solutions to these issues by considering reforms in industrial policy as well as enunciating a lucrative tax-subsidy package to woo investors. This much sought after destination by the domestic and foreign tourists is looked at with magnifying lenses and nervousness by all investors except the land sharks.

Active to oppose

The advocacy and activism for opposing each and every project in the name of environment and identity paints a picture that everything in Goa is "unwanted". Groups have mushroomed from villages to towns, from coastal beaches to hinterlands and from mining belts to industrial estates with the single banner of turning down anything that is being proposed.

Local opposition is understandable in situations where the damage to local interests is visible. It would be a deliberate suicide if Goa and Goans attempt to locate economic development in the perfume of drugs, wine, gambling, casinos and trafficking in women and children. We have dug this pit, not understanding sustainable long-term tourism development. This is the picture of Goa sold internationally and silence would be abetment to the imminent suicide. Though there is proliferation of industrial estates in rural areas, the category of industries granted permission have not contributed to the gainful employment of locals. The Goa Industrial Development Corporation has considered itself primarily as a property broker rather than agent of industrial development. Unregulated mining largely with the entry of non-traditional players has raised question marks due to the damage to environment, agriculture, horticulture and traditional perennial sources of water. The real estate boom totally independent of the domestic customers and users also raises questions on its utility. Citizen and community intervention including all forms of protest is not only understandable but also desirable.

Development means Propositions

Of late, thoughtless protests and armchair negativism is the order of the day. This is observed for every public or private project resulting in the emergence of "Advocacy" against each and every developmental project as the booming industry in Goa. Print, electronic and social media also thrive on such protests and corner agitations which receive disproportionate media recognition.

Today, Municipal Solid Waste Management is a burning problem for Goa. It is the waste that civilians create and not the government. This issue cannot be addressed without scientific collection, treatment and disposal of the waste. The problem will remain unresolved if everyone opposes the establishment of facilities to handle the garbage and waste. The similar situation would be with reference to medical waste. The wisdom we exhibit is to oppose without making any other alternative proposition. In a similar way, there is opposition to micro industry belts in villages and eco-tourism initiatives in environmentally fragile areas. Our attitude to agriculture, horticulture and animal husbandry is also negative and we propagate that these sectors would be always unprofitable. Provision of land for education hub, I.T. Park, Food procession zone and even housing also invites opposition. We are impatient to listen to planners and technocrats. Every village group feels that opposition to any development project is in the service of the Lord.

A few days back, I observed a NGO, supposedly tied to environmental causes pressurising law enforcement agencies to drive out street women and children taking shelter on open lands near the bus stands claiming that such temporary shelters of destitute families is the cause of plastic menace and dirt in the town. The NGO was well equipped with the local TV crew to gather media mileage for this social or environmental activism. Little do we realise that the generation of plastic waste is done by all of us and it is the street women and children who contain the spread in their own limited way. For us plastic is waste, for them it is source of livelihood. Driving out migrant women and beating migrant street children is not the solution for dealing with plastic waste. The solution could lie if we establish a vendor mechanism for plastic waste as we have for unused paper along with reduced use and reuse of plastic materials.

Taking this argument further, Goans derive pleasure by holding that thefts, robberies and crimes are due to migrants. In reality, these acts are not possible without insider abetment. Unemployment, greed for fast money, dependence on gambling, alcohol and drugs has drawn our youth to petty crimes is a sad reality which needs to be digested. We can shut it off at our own peril. The incidents in Goa of murder of parents, grand-parents and close relatives for money involved our youth, not migrants. The negativism and hatred cup of Goans against the migrants overflows. The sooner we halt this and move towards a rational understanding of the migration scenario would do us good.

The climate of merciless massacre of any proposition or plan of development without offering alternatives could give the status of investment-foe and investment-rival capital of India to Goa. The government can work on reforms in policies and financial incentives to encourage Goan investors as well as from outside. It is for the intellectual and thinking community to ensure that Goa is not crucified at the altar of negativism. Critical appreciation and rational analysis is always welcome. What needs to be guarded is the movement towards nihilism

With "Goenkarponn" and identity being stretched to unsustainable and unreasonable levels, a long eclipse has cast a lengthy shadow on development variables such as investment, employment, output, income and infrastructure in Goa. People and specially youth who desire to stay in Goa are worse off and going through hard days. Those who find employment in government and government-aided sectors enjoying insulation from market forces and shocks are an exception and would always be better off.

Identity is brought centre stage in social discourses and political debates. Development seems to lose the battle to what is termed as Goa's "unique identity". There is no serious thought on development and what one witnesses is thoughtless contest on identity. Every general election is a festival to resurrect and expound on this 'special Goan identity' and kill the much needed debate on development. As a result, Goa loses the developmental race as well as the identity tournament.

If any Indian State has to be nominated for an award for people's opposition to any type of development or any project or any growth plan, Goa will not face any competition.

It is only development which can retain identity. Goans have developed an attitude of looking outside the State and overseas for opportunities. This is not an unwelcome trend. The annoying and disturbing trend is to look at Goa as a retreat destination and retirement heaven by Goans themselves and to ensure that it is maintained likewise to serve the cause of Goa's identity. An attitude bordering on duplicity is to glorify that a Goan is global and should enjoy unfettered migration to any part of India and the world and in the same breath demand that immigrants to Goa should be thrown out.

Social welfare schemes are mechanisms to iron out the creases of development. They are answers to the question-marks of the challenged, underprivileged and senior citizens. They cannot be looked at as drivers of growth and moving the wheels of development.

Goa should not emerge as the negative NGO capital of India. Goans should also learn to weed out RTI activism and activists from becoming ganglords. The people should swing the debate to development from identity. The fear of loss of identity, language and culture puts the politicians, bureaucrats and planners in a comfort zone and gives power to caste and religious leaders to drown the people in the sea of ignorance.

Goa Business DNA

It is generally accepted that an average Goan shows undiluted preference for job and employment as opposed to business and self-employment. Under the work category the first choice of the Goan is for government service so much so that youth employed in private sector consider themselves to be unemployed till they get a posting in government. The next best choice is overseas employment which explains the presence of Goans all over the globe. The limited few whose option is business get tied exclusively to trading, tertiary services and calling which involves minimum of processing activity such as mining, restaurant business, liquor and bakery. Examples of Goan business tending towards core manufacturing are rare. Even established business families show no signs of plunging into major or ancillary industrial manufacturing. Goa has business families but cannot boast of a single industrial family like Kirloskars, Bajaj, Garware etc.

A profile of investment of surplus resources indicates the strong fondness of Goans for bank deposits. Shares, debentures, property and other assets are hardly on the agenda under the investment portfolio. This is the major factor explaining the low credit-deposit ratio of the banking sector in Goa.

I am making an attempt to construct the DNA of Goa business. Goa business throws a distinctive genetic code. These are set of traits and attributes acquired over a period of time which explains "why are we what we are". We may want things to be different but our wish-list cannot become a reality in the short-run. The DNA reflects the core competencies, investor psychology, perceived fears and dreams, family influences, social structure and location challenges of the community. It is the combination of all this which goes in the formation of the business DNA of a community.

Historically, Goa has been a trading location with a natural port and good network of inland waterways coupled with rail connectivity. The 450 years of Portuguese rule in Goa reinforced culture of trading along with the tradition of government service. Goans migrating all over for education and employment due to opportunities famine at home became an inevitable part and parcel of lifestyle. The attributes that the locals imbibed rightly or wrongly could be summarized as under:

- **Paramount importance to safety and security:** This explains the manner of how Goans distribute or invest the surplus resources and remittances. The same factor throws light on the aversion to risk-taking and risk-bearing indicating that entrepreneurship is something unnatural to the genetic code of a Goan.

- **Quick and immediate returns:** Business enterprise development of locals is largely in activities where the gestation period of payback is less than twelve months and in a few cases extends to 24 months. Probably it is the DNA which holds back the top traditional business houses of Goa to diversify into any segment where the gestation period is high.

- **Skill bias:** Somehow technical skills have not mixed well in the DNA. As a result, the preferred occupations and business enterprises are those involving minimum technical skills.

- **Owner presence:** The writ of owner attendance on the business campus dominates the DNA. Probably, this is the reason why Goan business does not walk on the track of scalable model. Owners are not keen in multiplying their successful business enterprises in different towns of Goa. We hardly see trading outlets of Goan businessmen at more than one location. Of late, a beginning is made to scale up by bakery units such as Pastry Palace, Monginis and restaurants such as Tato, Bhonsle, Bhingui. In the field of education, Bhatikar, Amonkar, Surlakar are brand names but at single locations.

Multiple locations and campuses is somehow unpalatable to the Goa business DNA. It is not a surprise that successful businessmen do not give a thought of crossing over to the two-tier towns such as Ratnagiri, Kolhapur, Hubli, Belgaum, Mangalore in neighbouring states.

- **Business thirst:** The DNA does not exhibit an insatiable "greed" for expansion and the kick of doing business just for the sake of business. The thirst gets quenched fast and satisfaction sets in early. Enough and no more is ingrained in the mindset.

As a parting point, let me say that the DNA can be changed over a period of time. Changes in demography and economic environment will modify the genetic code of business. Governments and public policy can transplant a new DNA. Educational programmes with added focus on skills and entrepreneurship could be also inputs in the planting process.

Section 3.

Developmental Delusions

The section on development delusions elaborates on Mining, Tourism and Casino industries. Casinos which are often described as the centre of tourist attraction has received much attention from the authorities despite people's objection. Unfortunately, sex crime and drug peddling is becoming the new normal. The author explains the repercussions of such shift and has identified the loopholes which need a fixture.

Tourism in Goa: A SWOT Analysis

Like agriculture, horticulture and fisheries which are regarded as primary occupations based on factor endowments, tourism industry is a gift of nature to Goa. If we fail to understand this simple wisdom and abuse the free bequest, no amount of investment in tourism infrastructure would retain the advantageous position of this tiny state on the west coast of India. Leave aside the longing of the domestic and foreign tourist to visit Goa again and again; there is much desire to make Goa as a second home. It is no wonder that a Goan is reluctant to leave Goa. Those who have migrated cannot erase Goa from their heart, mind and dreams. Something about Goa is magical. It is a sprinkle of the eight F's---- Food, Feni, Fun, Festivals, Forests, Friendly-nature, Football, Folk music and dance. The harmonious community mix gives a different colour to Goa from the rest of India, but the over advertisement and bombardment of communal harmony is a pointer that Goa is losing its community melody. We take to aggressive marketing to prove something when something is not or when we are on the verge of losing the prized value.

As Goa loses the primary natural gifts due to neglect and environmental degradation as a result of reckless exploitation for short-term profits, the state cannot afford to lose the natural advantage of tourism. Tourism is a strong economic driver for growth, employment and self-employment. By itself, it cannot cause harm to environment and culture. Tourism can expand market for horticulture, handicrafts, entertainment, fisheries, performing arts, hotel, hospitality and health industries if proper linkages are planned.

Brand Goa is the unique strength of tourism industry. The brand image of Goa as a destination is extremely strong. Most of the stakeholders comprising the travel and tourism industry are of the strong opinion that the industry has not benefited from the international road shows held at frequent intervals. It is Brand Goa which draws tourists and the monies spent on international road-events have no incremental effect on the traffic. Casino gambling, drugs and the picture of Goa as a garbage paradise hits the Goa Brand. The brand strength is getting further erased and diluted with politicians and their fringe elements making inroads rewriting social harmony and liberal lifestyle that is integral part of Goan.

Goa accounts for 14% of foreign tourist arrivals in India. 30% of the local population is engaged directly and indirectly in tourism related activity. Nearly 90% of the tourist arrivals are handled by the small and medium enterprises (SMEs) and the star category of hotels account for around 10%. However, the star category makes the major contribution to the revenue of the government from the tourism industry. This is to a large extent because of unreported, underreported or unaccounted transactions of the SMEs. The contribution of the tourism industry is also assessed from the outlets it creates to the growth of the tertiary sector. Due to the demand generated by the tourism industry, people have moved to higher social status as entrepreneurs and self-employed in the tourism value chain.

If the "sun, sea and sand" was the major asset of Goa's tourism, its overexploitation has made it as the major liability for future. North Goa is a concrete forest with clear signs of non-sustainability. No further in-depth studies are needed on this issue. The conflicts between locals' v/s migrants; locals' v/s tourists and the worsening law and order are pointers. The perception that control and monitoring on drugs would mean an end of tourism shows that the growth is vulgar and not consistent. Dirty beaches and expensive internal road transport (taxis) is the negative feedback from the tourists. The falling land use and land cover under the traditional cocoanut cultivation due to quick gains perceived in alternative uses is a permanent cost of tourism.

The weakness of tourism also arises from the failure to generate qualified and trained local human resource to meet the growing requirements of the hotel industry particularly in the production i.e. Food & Beverage slots. This is largely due to the poor availability of training facilities and the eligibility norms of admissions to such vocational programmes which mandate pre-educational qualifications. As a result, the local dropouts from educational system prefer to take the route to Middle East and Europe by completing internships with SMEs in tourism industry. The weakness of Goa's tourism industry lies in the reality that the industry is not confident of tomorrow. This means that despite the brand image, the industry has not reached into a self-propelling stage.

The tourism industry is facing a serious business threat. Though domestic tourist inflow has increased, the foreign tourist component offers no consolation. The 1990s saw the start of European & Scandinavian charter flights. From 80 charter flights, the figures increased to reach a boom of around 1062 in 2002. This has slumped to 180 charters in 2013-14. In-bound charter flights are facing decline, showing no signs of stable growth. The fall in the European charter flights was offset by the rise in Russian flights which crossed the 1000-mark in 2014-15. In the recent years the commitment is not reassuring.

Global recession could be one reason. At the same time, there seems to be a destination competition with Thailand, Sri Lanka and Malaysia becoming the most preferred. The tourist visa cost which is around 104 pounds per person makes it unfavourable for Goa as a destination choice. Goa has also taken a hit due to the unease on account of 'culture extremism'. There is a system failure to communicate expectations of the votaries of culture in a decent and dignified style. **A section of Goans are using culture as an "atom bomb" to destroy the culture of tolerance, harmony, creativity and freedom of choice.**

The irreversible damage to coastal ground water resources due to sewage and plastic waste is an eye-opener. The water contamination is complete in North Goa and particularly the Calangute-Baga-Candolim-Sinquerim belt. Many perceive an airport at Mopa as a threat to the tourism industry in South Goa. Let me submit, that if Mopa airport at all poses a threat to tourism, it cannot engulf only South Goa and keep North Goa untouched.

The opportunities are immense only if the fallen image of Goa is renovated. The perception that ***"Goa mein kuch bhi kar sakta hai"*** will strike the slow death of tourism. We need to move beyond the beach-church-temple circuit into waterways, waterfalls, villages, lakes etc. Opportunities in Business, Health, Adventure, and Heritage are to be harnessed. Maintaining forests intact as tourist products, we need to develop the non-coastal hinterland towns for tourism accommodation and the value chain.

The Government has appointed consultancy firm to prepare the master plan for tourism. The master plan should look "inside Goa"-- the more the planners look inside, the tourism will benefit the locals. The 'Make-in-Goa' should be modified into 'Made-by-Goa' because anybody can make-in-Goa. Even the Russians are doing it.

Casino Industry, Tourism and Economic Growth

The projection of the tiny State of Goa, well known for its natural and human assets for sustainable tourism as a casino destination continues to be a controversial issue. The local government seems to solidly back the casino stakeholders recognizing it as a prime mover of tourism and source of public revenue. With legalized casino gambling (gaming), the moral opposition to such gambling is gradually on the wane. The 'disagreeableness' to casinos appears to diminish with the argument that we need to provide all types of opportunities to tourists on vacation. At the same time, as the casino gambling popularity grows, the opposition also breeds as it is claimed to erode vitals of the community. In soft territories like Goa, the gaming regulatory mechanisms fall miles short to exercise effective control to protect customers, employees and environment. This 'safe heaven' perception and reality for professional gamblers and operators multiplies the threats of crime, criminal gangs, money laundering and social degradation.

Keeping the social fall out and moral implications aside, let's attempt to understand the casino industry in context of economic growth and material well-being of the local community. Contribution to public revenue through taxation and fees is one major input on which government support to casino industry seems to be justified. The Goa government is currently caught in acute fiscal deficit and badly requires revenue from whatever sources irrespective of any meritorious grounds. The issue on which the government needs to come clearly is on the quantum of revenue mobilized from casino industry and its areas of utilization. If this revenue is channelized towards education and social welfare schemes, the end use could mollify the attack as the source is socially regarded as not respectable.

Growing unemployment is a foremost challenge. The patronage to casino industry is sought as it generates direct and indirect employment opportunities. The employment is mainly in the area of security guards, gaming staff and technical manpower. In the absence of concrete data, it is not clear whether the casino industry in Goa has generated employment for locals and reduced the unemployment in the neighbourhood. There are employment opportunities but it is not ascertained that the workforce has come from the local areas. The indirect employment is through the demand created for hotel services and taxi operators. Whether casino industry results in more local sales in hospitality, entertainment, handicrafts and retail trade depends on the type of casino customers i.e. locals, domestic tourists and foreign vacation travellers. This data will throw light on the incremental customers boosting local sales. There are strong possibilities of casinos "cannibalizing" into other businesses whereby the spill over multiplier would hardly function. The money spent in casinos is money not spent at other markets and locations. The footfalls in casinos are drain on tourist falls at other sites and localities. A customer in restaurant and entertainment section run by casino will suck the customer from moving to other restaurants and recreational centres. It is such studies which will examine whether casino gaming industry contributes to actual growth or results in mere 'transfer' growth.

We are all aware that in a casino, players cannot alter the advantage of the operators. However, the propensity for gaming and gambling exists. Despite better and sane alternatives of tourism, we are also choosing to promote tourism by making the society "stupid". Such a course would have been on a strong standing if there were possibilities of neighbouring states robbing Goa's tourism flow by encouraging casino industry in their states. The current cross-border status is free from casinos, which means there is no potential of tourist theft or diversion by other states on account of gaming industry. This is a factor which could be weighed whilst making an assessment on requirement of casino industry in Goa for domestic tourists. For the international tourist, there are dream casino locations and the possibility of tuning Goa for casino gaming is the rarest of rare exception from foreign vacation seekers.

To put it straight, the issue for Goa cannot be onshore versus offshore casinos. The critical question is whether casino industry should be an integral and inseparable part of Goa's tourism vision. What are the motivations of visitors to Goa and will the effect on quality and family tourists be salutary or negative with casino operators positioning the land of sand, sun, waterfalls, forests, heritage and tranquillity as a paradise for professional gamblers.

In Goa, we abound in alcohol. There is easy access to drugs. There is buzz of commercial sex activity. We top all this with an oligopoly market of casino gaming. All this aggregated may be giving immediate windfalls with insolvable challenges for the future of tourism and overall economic growth of the state. If Goa is going to provide a permanent seat to the casino operators in the state by developing it into a hub, we will have to discard the notion of gambling being immoral and sin activity. Presently, academicians and researchers are almost practicing untouchability with no research output coming out on this legalized gambling which can serve as basis of public policy. There are studies highlighting debts, depression, suicides and bankruptcy but no business and economic studies in respect of the industry in the state.

Casino is more popular with the politicians than the people. There are no scientific studies detailing economic benefits such as contribution to government, local employment and ancillary benefits. Analytical data on the customer profile will provide clarity on the need-based argument for tourism. No authority can vouch on whether the casino operators are fully utilizing the banking channel or any secret channels in their cash management. No public policy and effective regulatory mechanism can evolve in the absence of accurate data on these aspects. Like any other industry, all aspects of casinos should be in public domain to guard against social disruption and economic dislocation. There are already indications that the casino lobbies have turned masters and the politicians cum governors are meek followers of the gambling 'gurus'.

Casinos:
Jackpot or blindness for Goa

Goa, a brand by itself for its natural charm and non-bothering attitude of its people who are known all over for their art of blending work and leisure can very comfortably sustain the tourism industry and its economy without the perils associated with casino industry which is sought to be bestowed with respectability by substituting gambling with gaming. Though, politically a State, administratively two Districts, a total population of around 15 lakhs which is not even 40% of the population of a district in any other state of India is otherwise like a town.

Six floating casinos in the river Mandovi and a couple on-shores is a guarantee for instability of economy and employment. In addition, it is extremely hazardous for the political and social health of this tiny State. The threat is also of Goa losing its core brand components. There are agreeable and suitable options for employment and growth in agriculture, fisheries, dairy, knowledge industry and services sector considering the human and youth potential of the State.

The proponents of casino gambling (gaming!) consider it as a part of the leisure and entertainment sector—like amusement parks, water sports or movie theatres. Those who support casino gambling generally do not see it as a moral issue and are indifferent to the long-term irreversible ills associated with it. The opponents are less unified in their opinions. Some disapprove of gambling on religious grounds. Others are suspicious of the industry which recruits and feeds thugs, cheats and shady politicians. Still others express caution as accessibility to casino gambling destroys youth and families as the lifestyle of gambling and complementary evils of prostitution and drug trade sound normal economic pursuits. There are few others whose opposition is restricted by the NIMBY factor---'not in my backyard'.

Costs & Benefits

A detached and unemotional review of casino industry would throw light on the benefits of this economic activity. The contribution to the public exchequer is sizeable in terms of license fees and taxes. The argument for heavy taxation gets emboldened as gambling is perceived to be 'anti-social'. Hence, for the government it turns out to be politically safe route to mobilize revenue for public welfare projects. The casino tycoons also attempt to wash off the alleged sins through saintly investments in schools, hospitals and social welfare programmes. They also clothe their promotions and advertising by supporting cultural organizations, artists, police and fire emergency services earning advantage of being a socially responsible corporate. The Goa Casino Operators hit the headlines welcoming Shree Ram Lalla Prathishatha at Ayodhya in their promotional campaigns.

The direct employment in the industry and the support to other businesses are the other main gains to the economy. Casinos are known to create entry-level job opportunities at fairly good compensation packages. Hence, this could be a good option to be encouraged where there is either chronic unemployment or alternative employment opportunities are difficult to be created.

The direct cost of casino operations is the burden put on the governments to address the cancer of gambling, organized crime, drug trade and prostitution. This is a heavy load as it is potent to derail social growth and harmony. The indirect cost is the growth of unaccounted wealth and opportunities of money laundering. The opportunity cost is the local hotels, restaurants and tourism service operators losing business as casino gambling competes with these genuine and stable businesses. Tourists and others glued to casino gambling are lost as customers to local hotels and stores. It is tested that other business owners in the neighbourhood suffer from the loss of business on account of casinos. This could be true of smaller locations like Goa rather than other big-sized States.

Casino and tourism

The issue is whether the marriage between casino gambling and tourism will be an economic success story of Goa. To understand this, the government should be ready with data on local employment in the casino industry which is presently believed to be not positive and encouraging. If casino is argued to be supporting tourism, it is very important to have data on family tourism. What goes on in the casino is adult entertainment which drains family tourism. Gambling invariably gives a shot in the arm to organized crime and it is for the government to assess its preparedness to deal with it.

It is well understood that casinos survive because of problem gamblers and because of people for whom gambling has become an addiction. People come with finances to lose. The goal is not to win money. It's addiction to stay in the game. It is referred to as "playing to extinction".

A Goan going to Les Vegas is not a compulsive gambler. But, here he could be, he will be. A casual visitor is not an issue but casinos would collapse if customers are just casual. If this argument is accepted, casinos cannot build local economy. It functions as a parasite which could set forces of local economic slowdown culminating in economic distress, domestic violence and crime.

The question therefore is--- Will Goa hit the jackpot in economic growth or tumble down losing everything it stands for? I would say it's never too late to find a better way.

Drugs- has Goa crossed the line of control

Deaths of youth at the Electronic Dance Music (EDM) site lit up the mountain of drug trade in the state of Goa challenging the international image of the tiny bountiful state as a pious, serene, cultured and safe destination. There is no shade of doubt now that the tranquil land of sun, sand, forests and historical heritage is infested with drug trafficking. As a location of traders, peddlers and consumers the state has traversed too far and crossed the line of control. Drugs are seen from the Northern tip of Ashwem and Morjim (Pedne) to the Southern slant at Palolem and Galgibaga.(Canacona). The presence is also experienced on the college campuses throughout the state.

No illegal trade can flourish without the police-trader-politician nexus in any part of the world. The government puts the blame on the victims as it is their free choice to consume or stay away from the narcotic substances. The police and anti-narcotics officers shifted the onus on the people to adduce proof of drug traders. The team of doctors at the apex government hospital brought discredit to their Hippocratic Oath whilst conducting medical examination of youth doused under influence of drugs. They almost resigned themselves to be tools in the hands of the government and the illegal traders by keeping their judgment and autopsy report opaque and inconclusive. All this is evidence enough that the government is cold and remorseless.

With or without EDM, Goa is a hot pot of drug retail. In today's age, it would be imprudent to look at drugs exclusively from the cultural or moral lens. From the beginning, the base of Goa's tourism has been all legal and officially authorized economic activity. With comparative natural advantages and liberal lifestyle, Goa emerged as a preferred destination for the international and domestic tourist. The reckless expansion of beach tourism coupled with the failure to harness available alternatives in terms of heritage, rivers, forests, adventure and hinterlands has made Goa to lose the competitive edge. Largely, out of panic of falling tourist traffic, we are now inserting an illegal base for tourism industry through casino gambling, drugs and prostitution. These are the black markets which provide temporary windfalls to hotels but are definitely not sustainable tourism models for benefiting all the stakeholders by ensuring the trickle-down effect.

Illegal markets and businesses are attractive propositions to police in terms of kickbacks and to politicians for the money spin. Once these illegal markets reach monstrous proportions, they tend to control the politics of the region. Logically, smaller communities and regions are easy prey. In drug commerce, around 85% of income goes to the kingpins. The poor locals get some boon. The consumers or customers are captive as they have no remedy against supply of substandard or spurious goods. No complaints can be filed against cheating and impure products. Illegal markets are a seller's paradise and buyer's hell. The negative impact is high on economies and would be evident in different ways.

As drug business establishes its roots, crime and violence is perceived to be a normal acceptable phenomenon. Public spending would be necessitated in expensive health care. Losses in human productivity would creep gradually. Finally, it becomes a region unfriendly for investment. What was earlier sought to be justified or ignored for tourism and hotel occupancy turns out to be the cancer giving a fatal blow not only to tourism but to legal economic activities.

To the Goa Minister who says "the show must go on", and to the Chief Minister whose pet pharse 'Bhivpachi goroz na' (Nothing to fear), it is hightime to engage in effective and purposeful consultation with the stakeholders. The industry is disturbed over the 'flop season' at peak time. In general, the occupancy rate is less than 50% in hotel industry. The shack operators are distressed with the low foot falls. The other related businesses are unhappy. The talk is that without promotions, Goa used to have tourists flow which catered to the interests of all. Today, with the so called promotions and foreign jaunts of the ministers and their cronies, the industry is finding it difficult to smile. It is a pointer that something is basically amiss.

Goa still enjoys the luxury of choosing legal markets and above-board alternatives for boosting tourism and answering the problems of the tourism industry. A deliberate choice has to be made to keep tourism delinked from gambling, drugs and prostitution. The argument is not the traditional one of morals and culture. If we do not make the conscious choice, the days of international tourist flow will wither away very fast. The domestic family tourist arrivals will also be numbered. The show will come to a grinding halt for legal tourist stakeholders. For the illegal markets whose survival is through connivance with greedy politicians and corrupt police, nothing matters and anything is suffice.

Casino wins, Tourism loses

The Indian illegal gambling market is quite intensive and extensive. However, the legal casino gambling (being legal, it is now elevated to gaming) is allowed only in two states of India i.e. Sikkim and the always blessed Goa. I am told that there is only one casino in Sikkim. Goa takes pride in hosting seventeen casinos so much so that the capital city of Goa appears to dance on the banks of river Casino, River Mandovi being hardly visible. Goa is now known to the world as the casino jewel of India.

The casino gains

Goa was famous for its local brew "feni" and Goans were quizzed on wine and liquor under the belief that it was natural for the locals to stay drowned under the influence of these juices. To some extent, this was tolerable except for the way in which a Goan was sought to be represented in Indian cinema. The image of this State is of fun loving people tied to the bottle with sparsely clad women enjoying dance and the common thread of idleness and laziness binding all.

Goa is equally a place with a rich mosaic of culture blended with communal harmony. This tranquil, vibrant and friendly cosmopolitan human environment is unique to Goa which is rare to find in any other State of India. This natural and spontaneous vein in the life of Goans is not celebrated though this appears to be the prime reason for domestic and international tourist traffic. This lack of understanding made our government to legalise gambling with a view to attract the high spending tourists and give a boost to the tourism industry which is undoubtedly a mainstay of our economy.

The traditional liquor industry is one which we have inherited. It has backward and forward linkages. The roots of these linkages percolate to villages and the traditional occupations. Casino gaming is an invited drug which has made the sexy and enticing river Mandovi ugly and polluted. The entry of casino gambling has damaged the positioning of Goa in the domestic and foreign market. It has contributed to intensify drug market, prostitution including child abuse and crime associated with this form of gambling. The casino trade is fuelled by unearned incomes, dividends from speculative transactions, fast kickbacks from corrupt deals and windfalls in the hands of public officers, politicians and professionals. Like a land fill for untreatable solid waste, the casino turns out to be a slot and management centre for such "waste" and unaccounted money.

Let us look at the realities. Having created a devil to support the tourism industry for which we have natural endowments, we now feel that there is no alternative except to sleep with the evil spirit. The direct employment generation in this sector is around 5000, out of which 30% are locals. There are indirect dependents in terms of retail business. The revenue to the local government is around Rs. 85 crores i.e. almost half of what the government lost due to removal of VAT on petrol. It is advisable to earn from petrol as opposed to business which directly spins crime and puts pressure on law enforcement agencies. It is largely the domestic tourist who frequents the casino as compared to the foreign tourist. The casino driven tourist does not add value to the overall economic activity of the region except marginal contribution to the occupancy rate of resorts. Casino trade has the larger burden of the illegal 'extortion tax'. The trade is an animated centre of black money and acts as the reservoir for election funding as well as all illegal businesses.

The lost kingdom

With the siege of the casinos, Goa has lost to value what it is and what it means to be. The image of the local population in the rest of the country is exactly opposite of what we are. Goans despite high morals and ethics are discredited. Goa is looked as the land for enjoyment without restraints and the friendliest destination for all vices. You name the vice and Goa will not disappoint.

This poses a big danger to the security of tourism industry and to sustainable tourism. There is an urgent need to look at this scenario as the State cannot afford to lose despite natural gifts, diverse culture, rich heritage and the hospitable population. Tourism can provide ample opportunities for developing occupations and providing self-employment in the hinterlands and also the coastal belt. The short-cuts of providing opportunities which appease to the baser and meaner instincts of people should be stopped. Tourism is not about gambling, drugs and prostitution. Even if assumed to be so, Goa should be looked as a destination for something different.

Why everyone wants to visit Goa? Why do we have repeat visitors? Why is Goa a preferred destination? Going a step further, why do outsiders i.e. domestic and foreigners desire to own a space in this territory? This is not a normal tendency with other locations. We need to seriously know this so that we offer to our tourists, the Goa they treasure rather than the slot machine and dice which spins money, crime, abortions and prostitution.

We can change the image of Goa in one stroke. This is by repealing the Public Gaming Act. The travel and tourism industry should give the desired push and exercise the big pull in their own self-interest.

Tourism- Regaining The Lost Paradise

In any season, Goa is a paradise for an insider. There is no reason why the same should not hold relevant for an outsider who is seeking a 'vacation home' away from home. The trend of dwindling number of foreign tourist arrivals despite the marketing drives and promotions indicates ineffectiveness in the exercises. The claims of the tourism stakeholders that promotions have degenerated into ministerial and bureaucracy oriented foreign jaunts seem plausible. It could also be that today's Goa is no longer what it is perceived by the foreign vacation seekers. Added to this, could be emerging locations and offerings in the rest of India. It appears that the high-spending tourist no longer considers this tiny land as attractive and adding value. Even the low-spending tourist is gradually turning the back due to superior competitive locations.

The domestic tourist footfalls are substantial. The government and the industry need to design, build, operate and market a wide spectrum of sight-seeing and stay packages to engage the tourist for extended durations. It does not look that the tourism industry and the government has positioned the band of offerings---- hinterland, village, river, historical, heritage and forest. Infrastructure development through public and private investment is required for this dispersal. There should be a deliberate strategy to lace up this wide range of tourist circuits with local cuisine, handicrafts and performing arts. Such approach will ensure benefits to locals in terms of employment, entrepreneurship and income.

Sand, Serenity to gambling

Goa started well making its print on the international map as a destination of "sun, sand, serenity, harmony, privacy with the salt of Goan hospitality". Now, due to overexploitation and lack of vision, the tranquil beaches have become ponds of waste and filth. The entire coastal belt resembles a desert of concrete. It's equally a jungle of drugs, paedophile and sex trade. Definitely, once the soul of the location is destroyed, just the flesh, groomed artificially and spruced up through cosmetic surgery can no longer lure the visitor. Finally, these locations will receive the tourist as deserved by the current status of these locations.

Goa will be repeating the mistake yet again by positioning casino gambling as the main ingredient of the state's tourism dish. If casinos are made the critical component of what Goa offers, it will be the beginning of the end of tourism industry of Goa. The footfalls in casinos hardly percolate to the wider stakeholders. The visitor is chained within, totally centered on the elusive casino honey. The casino orientation kills family tourism. The employment in this enterprise is less of locals. There were reports of over 800 casino employees from North-Eastern states lining up for registration as first time voters in the 2022 state assembly elections. This busts the myth of local employment leaving aside minor exceptions. It is a tragedy that the government and the tourism industry are destroying the natural and free assets available on a platter and putting their faith in risky assets like casinos which the investors can withdraw anytime. This is a dangerous gamble for the future of tourism industry in the state.

Roadmap

The Travel and Tourism Association of Goa (TTAG) has the roadmap to rejuvenate Goa's natural and backbone industry. Their inputs in the areas of infrastructure, transport, garbage management and branding are valuable. Being in trade, they know what is best for industry. The industry gets burnt when the footfalls fall. Recommendations in the sphere of transport are worth implementing as that will serve the interests of local population too. Probably, Goa is the only progressive state where the taxi services are refusing to harness technology. However, the wisdom needs to dawn that technology improves productivity of the service-provider. Goa also needs multiple transport options to locals as well as tourists. The public transport system in Goa can be described as most undeveloped in comparison to any state in Southern India. Similarly, garbage management and cleanliness has got derailed in entire Goa. Even if these two issues are addressed it would not only add value to tourists but also improve the quality of life of local population.

Branding, marketing and promotion are managed by agencies which are not Goan and therefore fail to understand "Brand Goa" that they profess to sell. The soul of Goa is absent in the menu card that they finally dishout.

Tourism is the natural industry of Goa. Goa's physical and human environment is endowed for providing leisure and comfort to tourists. What we require is planned spectrum of tourist circuits to engage the visitors. When we have the wheel for tourism gifted to this land, we are attempting to fit a totally different steering wheel recommended by consultants who know little of Goa's ethos and richness. In the bargain, the tourism stakeholders lose. Goa has lost, is losing further and could lose the natural advantage and free gifts forever.

Mining-Breaking the Jinx

The mining industry and iron ore exports of Goa which continued nonstop for over 50 years was brought to a grinding halt on grounds of sustainability and the need to maintain ecological balance in the exploitation of the natural resources. Equally strong was the argument of reckless mining and illegalities of different shades by the lease-holders. The concern for inter-generational equity in the exploitation of the non-renewable resource brought the issue of a cap on yearly extraction. It is difficult to pinpoint one clear reason for the forced closure of this economic activity which in the initial years after Goa's liberation was the major propeller of the state's economy.

Mine-owners are actually lease-holders and not owners of mines. However, the mind-set is of ownership or perennial lease. Extraction of iron ore by the lease-holders continued even after the expiry of the lease period. In many cases, the mandatory environmental clearances had lapsed. Instances of violation of environmental norms were rampant. Practically, no excavated mining site seems to have attempted closure as per the laws in force after completion of full extraction. The perception of the general public was that the entire mining lobby which includes the logistics providers had scant respect for laws. Fly by night operators entered the fray to make a fast buck making a mince meat of all regulations. All this would not be possible without the blessings of the administration and law enforcing public agencies. Everybody's greed to reap the golden eggs in the shortest possible time killed the goose.

Post-Shah quake

The Shah Commission report (2021) used strong words describing the mining operations in Goa as unrestricted, unchecked and unregulated which make exporters "richer and richer'. The Commission indicted the political executive and passed strictures on almost all the regulatory bodies i.e. Indian

Bureau of Mines, MoEF, Forest Dept., Mines Dept., and the Goa State Pollution Control Board. The aftermath of Justice M. B. Shah Commission report mainly on the menace of mining in Goa putting the scam worth at Rs. 35000 crore saw the then Chief Minister Manohar Parrikar ordering stoppage of mining in September 2012 as soon as the report was tabled before the Parliament. A petition filed by Goa Foundation was already pending for orders before the Supreme Court. It looked that the Chief Minister wanted to win the race with the judiciary and steal the thunder from the Supreme Court. The Ministry of Environment & Forests suddenly got up from the slumber to suspend the Environmental Clearances of 139 mining leases. Later, the Supreme Court struck the final blow by suspending the mining leases on account of violations detected by the Shah Commission. It looks that it was a game between the BJP ruled state government and the UPA at the centre, each working to checkmate the other and derive the mileage for acting on the illegalities and irregularities. This was immediately followed with an ex-parte order from Justice Aftab Alam ordering closure of the total economic activity related to mining. This intervention of the Supreme Court put the ball for restart of mining operations outside the ambit of both the governments.

It looks a contradiction that both the governments who took the lead to stop the mining operations immediately started to talk about resumption of mining. Both governments did it with lot of fanfare and drama but at the next moment got into a mode of mourning and grief over the revenue losses for the government and the plight of mining dependents. It took 3 years to break the standstill of 2012. The knot was released in September 2015 for the restart once the Supreme Court gave clearance for conditional resumption of iron ore mining. There was a cap of 20 million tons per annum for extraction. A prohibition was imposed for dumping of extracted iron ore outside the lease area. A condition for creation of Iron Ore Permanent Fund was imposed through accumulation of 10% of the sale proceeds of iron ore which is to be utilized for sustainable development and for the welfare of the people around the mining belt. Around 500 crore is collected and almost lying unutilized largely because the public authorities do not have an actionable plan in place.

This order delivered by the Bench of Justice A. K. Patnaik ensured only legal operations. There was no change in the status of mines. The leases stood expired in 2007, after the twenty year renewal period starting from 1987. The direction was for issue of fresh leases by the state government and fresh environmental clearance from the MoEF. This meant that no lease was subsisting beyond 2007. As a consequence, the extraction and export of iron ore from these leased lands (legally not on lease) for the period 2007-2012 was illegal and could not be said to belong to the private mine-owners. The state government decided to renew all these leases retrospectively subject to payment of stamp duty and the cess levied for iron ore extraction for the period 2007-12. Though the state was groaning under the mining ban, the Mines department recovered from mining companies around 900 cr as stamp duty and conversion fee for illegally dumping ore on agricultural lands. Public revenue looked to be the sole consideration of the government. Those who raised cudgels against illegal mining and particularly Goa Foundation held that all the mined iron ore during the stated period 2007-12, being illegally extracted (no subsisting lease) should be construed to be under government ownership. It was their contention that this would give a tremendous boost to the resource-strapped public exchequer resorting to unbridled public borrowings and free the people from additional tax burden.

The Goa Foundation has been under attack from the mining stakeholders including the government of being anti-development. In fact, the former Chief Minister of Goa, Manohar Parrikar is on record saying that the government will not be responsible for any attack on Claude Alvares, the critical human force behind the NGO. Goa Foundation is despised by all stakeholders who profit from mining. At the same time, it should put on record that the GF is actually doing the work of the government and that its actions have benefited the government in terms of revenue and also the people who consider themselves as victims of mining. If the liability of litigation is thrust upon the Goa Foundation, then so should be the asset for absorbing a slice of the private resources from sale proceeds of excavated iron ore to the public household. No government pleader could have done it better for the public exchequer than the GF in respect of this non-renewable natural resource of the state.

Renewals v/s fresh leases dilemma

The mining operations which partially commenced after the three years ban ran into rough weather once again in 2018 when Justice Madan B. Lokur speaking for the Supreme Court quashed the grant of 88 renewals of mining leases holding that the order of the court was for grant of fresh leases by the state government and fresh ECs by MoEF. The apex court directed that all mining operations should stop from 16th March, 2018 and commence only on grant of fresh leases, not renewals. The court did not find the exclusive revenue argument of the state government acceptable. The court was critical of the MoEF which was supposed to grant fresh ECs and not just lift the abeyance order of 2012. Holding that the second renewal of mining leases was hasty, the court opined that the real intention of the second renewal was to satisfy the avariciousness of the leaseholders. The court observed that the state government has done this with the full knowledge that the Government of India is introducing the auction route by inserting 10B in the MMDR Act. Further, knowing fully well that the promulgation of the Ordinance to this effect will be done by the President on 12th January, 2015, the state government rushed through the second renewal of leases from November 2014 to 12th January, 2015 in around three installments. The court was critical of the state government for pressing the accelerator to circumvent the policy of the Government of India. The Supreme Court set aside the directions of the Bombay High Court (Lithoferro v/s State of Goa) in the batch of petitions wherein the High Court opined that the renewal of lease also amounts to a new lease and further invoked the doctrine of promissory estoppel pursuant to the petitioners position by depositing the huge stamp duty with the state government. The Supreme Court directed the state government to grant fresh mining leases in accordance with the provisions of the MMDR Act.

This was the stalemate position. The state government could auction the leases to secure the best returns through the competitive bidding process. The state government was also toying with the idea of forming Mining Corporation. It was not clear whether the Corporation would engage itself into the core business of excavation and exports or only be an agency for conducting auction and competitive bidding. The experience of such government corporations in the coal sector was not at all salutary. There were also pleadings before the apex court that the Goa mining leases are of a different type and require a separate consideration. The observation of the Supreme Court that "the state government was not under any constitutional obligation to grant fresh mining leases through the process of competitive bidding or auction" (The Goa Foundation v/s M/S. Sesa Sterlite Ltd. 2018 para 149) raised grounds for alternative paths. But, no such corridors are elucidated in the order. For the start of mining operations, it was imperative that the state government grants fresh leases and further the MoEF considers the grant of fresh ECs. It is actually the domain of the state government and not the courts. The power of the courts is one of judicial review and to examine the executive action in terms of the Goa's Mineral Development Policy, the MMDR Act and the regulatory mechanisms.

Lokayukta blows hot

The report of the Goa Lokayukata (January, 2020) has come to the finding that the former Chief Minister Laxmikant Parsekar has violated the public trust and faith with impunity by granting renewal of leases to several mining lease holders. The Lokayukta passed strictures against two public functionaries--- Secretary (Mines) and Director (Mines Department) for violations of the provisions of MMDR Act with impunity and scant regard for the rule of law. The Lokayukta has recommended the filing of FIR by the State Anti-Corruption Bureau (ACB) and also directed the state government to entrust the investigation to CBI including their prosecution under the Prevention of Corruption Act.

Needless to say, that this report is recommendatory and will get a decent burial. The report itself admits that it is difficult to prove any pecuniary advantage but it is a clear abuse of official position to confer huge benefit to some of the mining lease holders. There is also a mention that none dared to name Shri Manohar Parrikar before the Lokayukata who as Chief Minister had also approved renewal to a few leases in November, 2014 which have been also quashed by the Supreme Court. The BJP government in the state and at the centre would have unfastened hell if any similar observations were recorded about the political opposition. By now, stories of arrests, custodial interrogation, Enforcement Directorate and Income-tax raids would have inundated the media.

Is it a futureless future?

All the stakeholders shed tears for the stoppage of mining. The government puts deadlines after deadlines for the commencement. Is Goa prepared for the re-start of mining? Assuming fresh leases are granted and fresh ECs are obtained, will the mining operations resurrect? The situation is almost like reviving from the dead.

The grant of clearance by the Supreme Court for transportation and shipping of iron ore out of Goa brought some cheer to the stakeholders and relief to the government. The permission was for royalty-paid iron ore if the mineral was mined before March 15, 2018. This in no way could be considered as a re-start of mining operations. This allows mining companies in the state to export the extracted ore. The moment this news flashed, the retrenched employees came up with the demand for re-instatement. The Goa Mining People's Front signaled that no activity will be allowed to commence before re-employment of workers. Some political outfits argued that the said ore being illegally mined, these dumps belong to the government and cannot be claimed by the mining companies and exporters. The matter as it stands today is the vexed problem of multiple vested interests.

- **Are the lease-holders ready?** Profitability of mining operations largely depends on the scale and volume. A low quantity may not be economical and feasible. The next important factor is the current prices in the international market. Australia and Brazil has huge quantities of good quality ore as compared to Goa. Our exporters have earlier tasted super high profits even for low quality ore. The sole motive was to make profits, no matter how and there were no qualms of putting law on backburner. Safety, environmental standards and damage control measures should form the integral part of extraction and logistics.

- **Are the service providers ready?** The barge owners would have to restore their fleet of barges in operational condition. The same is the issue of truck owners. Their preparedness to provide services at cost effective rates needs assessment and their demands should find acceptability. They are too many of them to be satisfied with the required volume and rates. The infrastructure at the port would need the tuning to provide the logistics.

- **Will auction and competitive bidding be acceptable?** The traditional and local mine-owners have the expertise as a consequence of their long experience but are no match for the muscle of the big players such as Vedanta, Jindal, and Adani. The internal politics and clash of business interests within the industry has also contributed to the stoppage of works. An acceptable formula would be required to be knit up because the local mining entrepreneurs may be forced to play a subservient role.

- **Is the administration prepared with regulatory mechanism?** The politicians and the bureaucrats were addicted to arm-chair kickbacks all these years and had made a complete mockery of rules and regulations. Many of these interests had dipped their hands in mining logistics. Future mining operations should not draw the public ire and the crushing rod of the Courts. This would necessitate the effective working of all regulatory institutions with transparent systems in place.

- **Are employees and the so termed 'mining dependents' geared up?** When an economic activity has to re-start after such a long duration of suspension, what is required is sensible, responsive and responsible approach from these stakeholders. The expectation is responsible bargaining resulting in win-win for the employees and owners.

A re-start of the mining operations in the state would not be as easy as it is thought to be. Auction, competitive bidding, government Mining Corporation, fresh lease renewals or leases in perpetuity etc are just different conduits. For the operations to commence on the ground and continue without abrupt interruptions, the stakeholders should be ready for the collective challenges.

The government has completed the bidding and auction of mining blocks. Now, the focus turns to feasibility and the actual commencement of operations.

Standing with Melauli-Sattari
(with inputs from Akbar Gaded)

The story of IIT in Goa has been one of opposition by locals whether it was at Sanguem or Canacona or Sattari. Any institution of higher learning, specialty and super-specialty courses should be welcome in Goa. Setting up of a national institute like IIT, apart from expanding educational opportunities also creates a nucleus which generates gainful employment and self-employment opportunities for locals. It gradually grows into a township generating demand for housing, retail, hospitality, health care, general education and a host of other allied services.

There could be local resistance at certain locations primarily due to economic reasons revolving around dispossession of agricultural land, usurpation of livelihood opportunities and existing arrangements of subsistence. It is a proved story everywhere that those whose lands have been compulsorily acquired by the government for public projects have turned fools and paupers. It is a rag to riches story of the sections who own lands in the periphery of the proposed educational centre as land values invariably shoot up. In addition, there are political and land sharks who acquire titles to land in such locations at the nick of time and get windfalls for the "wise" investment though done in clandestine manner.

Actually, the opposition is not to the centre of higher education or a national institute of learning. It is a struggle to protect ownership of land and opportunities of livelihood linked to the land sought to be acquired under a law which suffers from the vice of inequity for land losers. If the government can work out a win-win formula for small farmers, petty horticulturists and tenants dependent on the land, the resistance would just evaporate.

By adopting a policy of partial acquisition and retaining some fractional land area with the ownership rights to these sections, the government would promote equity and justice to the dispossessed. These land losers would than stand as equals with other beneficiaries and derive benefits of growing land values in the command area of the public project. Along with the monetary compensation, the land losers should be provided a partial compensation component in terms of built-up spaces in areas to be raised as commercial markets or housing of employees/faculty. It is with such built-in mechanisms that such projects can harness concrete benefits for the locals. Otherwise, the locals who are dispossessed of land, lose everything including their roots. Those in the periphery and investors flocking from outside have nothing to lose but only to gain from direct works and indirect spill overs of the project.

The crux of the issue at Melauli (Sattari) is the blanket grant of 10 lakh sq. meters of "Alvara" land and its transfer to the central government without any reference or consultation with the cultivators. These are the fields and plantations in possession of the villagers under the Portuguese Decree 3602 dated 24/11/1917. These lands form the base of their income, livelihood and employment. The Goa Land Revenue (Modification & Regularization) Act, 2007 has enunciated the procedure for grant of ownership title to the decree holders. The Goa Land Revenue Code was amended in 2017 to initiate the process of such grants after due process and payment of requisite fees to the government.

In the context of Sattari, it is pertinent to mention here that the Maratha rulers and Adil Shah had conferred rights of revenue collection on properties which are referred as "Mocasodari" and "Barrao". These revenue collectors of yesteryears stand sanctified as owners and no government has ever looked at the issue equitably and addressed the rights of tenants and sharecroppers on these lands. It is well known that these deemed owners wield tremendous political power and clout over all governments. However, when it comes to lands in possession of the masses in the village, it is annexed by the government without recourse to any due process. This is dictatorial, cruel and inhumane route chosen by the government to dispossess the villagers from the lands which they occupied and cultivated spreading generations. If this act is within the powers of the executive, then it is 'legalized robbery' with total disdain for the conditions of the poor and vulnerable villagers of Melauli- Sattari.

At the national level and particularly in the BJP ruled states, we have seen the abuse of power by the state instrumentalities in dealing with dissent and protests. Media is rife with reports of police misrule, crackdown on students, detention of activists, beating up of anti-CAA protestors and ransacking homes of those holding flags of dissent in states like Uttar Pradesh and Delhi. It is a matter of grave concern for people that the government of Goa and the ruling politicians are intolerant even to the feeblest protest of the poor and the dispossessed.

Though the hands of the politician are invisible per se, the locals and the people of Goa know the suave tricks and the dictatorial composition of the politicians. The locals bear the heat of the terror in this interior hamlet of Goa. At the same time, the unrestrained behaviour of the delinquent police officers is an assault on the fundamental and basic democratic right of speech and expression. This infringement on the primary human rights of the helpless, powerless and vulnerable sections needs to be taken up suo motu by the State Police Complaints Authority. This state known for its liberal and freethinking society rightfully expects suo motu cognizance from the higher judiciary on this marauding of democratic rights by the police. Goa should be insulated from joining the illegal and unconstitutional tracks laid down by police in other states and more specifically those ruled by the BJP.

IIT Learning:
Making land losers beneficiaries:

The story of providing a permanent campus for the Indian Institute of Technology (IIT-Goa) continued to stay inconclusive for over eight years. It started with the Laxmikant Parsekar led BJP government offering 225 acres at Dhargal, Pernem which was rejected by the MHRD which demanded 400 acres. Later, a 5 lakh square metre was identified in the village of Shristhal and Poinguinim in Canacona taluka but the locals raised strong objections. The Pramod Sawant led BJP government almost handed over around 10 lakh square metre of land to the IIT at Shel-Melaulim village in Sattari but had to finally retreat due to protest from farmers and inhabitants turning violent. We are now told that 7.5 lakh square metre at Sanguem will be finally the location of the IIT-Goa campus. The farmers and land losers are protesting with the government unlikely to relent as evident from the deployment of police force at the identified site.

The dance for land

The common thread in this dance for finding an acceptable and peaceful location for an all-India institute of higher learning is the threat of life-long loss of land resource facing the owners or occupiers of land. However, the protestors are hunted as a community opposing a national project. It is argued that establishment of IIT will open opportunities of employment for locals and also multiply prospects of enterprise in the command area. Further, it is argued that education being a non-polluting activity does not raise any environmental concerns. Those who oppose are sought to be categorised as anti-development.

The critical issue in all land acquisitions by the government is the permanent loss suffered by the land losers. They could be owners, occupiers, inhabitants, cultivators and dependents. As opposed to this, exactly contrary is the position of those whose lands do not come under the axe of the land acquisition. These groups suddenly get elevated as permanent beneficiaries of the project. For land losers, it is impoverishment for life. For those who retain their lands, it opens the window of riches for life. If this inequity is answered, the land acquisition will be fair, just and peaceful. Any such land acquisition would be welcomed and accepted.

In the initial years of post-liberation Goa, land acquisitions were not opposed or contested the way they are today. Stakeholders in land have learnt and tasted the bitter pill of this legalised land 'grabbing' by the government. Those whose lands were acquired for industrial estates got peanuts and the owners of lands in the neighbourhood reaped bumper profits. We are a witness to the stories of "rags to riches" of politicians and persons close to power on real estate acquisitions in the periphery of highways. We are also a witness to politicians building up fortunes as land investors with threatened land acquisitions.

First of all, it needs to be understood that none are opposing the IIT. The assumption that it is the duty of those who have vested interests in the land to permanently surrender their rights and benefits simply because IIT is a premier and prestigious academic institution is erroneous. Whether IIT or any other institution should be also accountable for the quantity of land it requisitions. We have the living examples of requisitioned lands lying idle and unutilised for over 25 years with institutions. Further, the government is one of the biggest 'zamindar' already holding idle lands. It continues to top it up with more land acquisitions of small landowners, cultivators and occupiers. There seems to be no accountability of the land already acquired and in possession of the government.

Revenue-sharing

IIT of today is not purely an academic enterprise. Lands put at the disposal of the IIT are also leased or sold to corporates for setting up economic and business establishments like shopping malls, superstores, restaurants, hotels, guest houses and recreation centres in the campus. It is true that IIT largely is an academic institution. But, the issue of land has social, economic and political manifestations. When the dispossession of land boils, the whole issue is bound to turn political.

It is under this background and the current context of land scarcity that the government should work out an innovative approach towards providing the land for any project. If the land losers are made permanent beneficiaries there would be no opposition or protests in augmenting the required land for public projects, national institutions or private industry. Just an upfront payment under the nomenclature of 'compensation' is a very poor consolation in the current context. The assurance of employment is vague and cannot be the quid pro quo for permanent dispossession of land.

For a projects like IIT, NIT, IT park, airport, public housing and similar economic activities along with the compensation package as provided under the Land Acquisition Act, 2013, the government and the project proponents should evolve a revenue-share alliance with land losers as a substantial chunk of land will be used for hotels, shopping malls, restaurants, eateries and residential complexes. The land losers should be provided a share in the lease rentals of these properties.

Stake in future profits

Another innovation could be in the form wherein the land owner retains the ownership rights on a fixed percentage of the land. A part of the land is brought under land acquisition and the balance is retained by the owner to be provided on lease. This arrangement provides an equitable option to the owner to renew the lease at increased rentals or sell the land at market prices in future. Such an arrangement protects the land owner from the permanent damage and at the same time puts the onus on the institution to act with financial responsibility. Such a procedure will automatically coerce institutions like IIT to prune their demands for land to actual requirement. The pride and majesty of IIT is not in the land it owns. Its prestige will be determined by human resource, research, placements and intellectual freedom.

Airport: One Enough, Two Not Yet

The issue of a second airport in Goa, should have been debated and analysed on financial feasibility, commercial considerations and overall economic growth of the State and the command area including the neighbouring district of Sindhudurg. Such a long-term project involving heavy investment and huge chunk of land resource cannot be converted into a North Goa versus South Goa dispute. At the same time, looking at the passenger traffic and cargo projections for the next ten years, we should have weighed the possibility of meeting the demand needs with modifications to the existing infrastructure arrangements at Dabolim as this approach would have caused the least disturbance to land and ecology. The way the debate headed coupled with the rash haste of the government has resulted in the loss of opportunity to take decisions based on solid economic reasons.

Airport is perceived as an attractive proposition by vocal opinion makers in the vicinity and the politicians. This polarised the matter to Dabolim versus Mopa. The echo for Dabolim turned loud. The hand of the hotel lobby from South Goa got visibility.

This glamorous arrival and departure station apparently seems to develop the employment and occupations of local communities. Having sold this, a retreat would mean that the government is not serious with the development of Pernem. There are better alternatives of expanding opportunities for people with minimum displacement but they were not appreciated and recognised.

The myths

Airport cultivates the development of local communities in the neighbourhood is a myth. It definitely creates the demand for new settlements and township for skilled and unskilled labour. Unless education, recruitment and training of locals are made an integral part of airport construction and development, locals remain untouched. The local landowners have to forcibly surrender their lands at the government rates and within a year the land values sky-rocket throwing the locals out of the land market. However, this can be harnessed to the benefit of local landowners only if the government implements a land acquisition policy wherein the government allows every landowner to retain 50% of their lands and acquires the balance. This enables the owners to take the benefit of market rates on completion of the airport project. This is how the government could be a catalyst to ensure that the benefits of public investment accrue to the locals. At a later stage, the locals themselves could be stakeholders in the projects which are necessitated due to the airport if they retain their ownership over land. This would be the stage when land is required to meet the residential requirements, warehousing, related airport services, educational institutions, business establishments, hotel industry and ancillary services. Failure to do this, results in dispossession and deprivation to the families who have contributed for the infrastructure project and supernormal gains to those land owners whose lands do not fall in the project area. This is the picture of Mopa and Pedne taluka today.

Since, Goa already has a reasonably good functional airport at Dabolim with expanded terminal and night landing facilities; a reliable, fast, hassle free road link from Canacona to Pernem and from the airport to all major talukas/industrial estates could be a booster for business, service sector and tourism industry of the State. Development of Pernem as a hub for education and performing arts along with good transportation network can prove to be more gainful to the locals than an international airport. If we want to be engulfed by the myth that only an airport at Mopa would open the door of development to this otherwise neglected taluka of Goa and nothing less than this is tolerable, then let us learn it by burning our fingers. The learning has dawned after the commissioning of the Greenfield project, Manohar International airport.

Another myth in circulation is of two airports----Dabolim and Mopa. Traffic projections show the low feasibility of Mopa airport even if the entire traffic of Dabolim stands diverted to the new centre. The State government has taken an assurance from the central government in writing that Dabolim would be retained at all costs. Such an undertaking does not bind the future governments lifelong from not taking a contrary view. The central government may very well oblige but passenger and cargo is not guided by the written assurances between these two governments. It will all depend on the operations and the business decisions of the investors. The present studies show that the splitting of traffic of the two airports will make both uneconomical. Take the case of government primary schools in Goa. Earlier governments were forced to give assurances on the floor of the Goa Assembly that the government will continue to run these schools irrespective of enrolment. We have now reached a situation wherein we have no alternative except to amalgamate due to dismal record of enrolment which in practical terms is a refined word for closure. The best option is one airport. If we want to go with the two airport model, we should not have done it without a development strategy in place to keep the two burners on fire.

Halt the hurry

The present airport at Dabolim would have served the needs of Goa without stress and strain for the next fifteen years. The airport was renovated with new terminals. The parking arrangement appeared to be a major hindrance, resulting in some chaos. This issue can be addressed without herculean efforts.

Traffic projections and the present state of the major economies of the world do not send warm signals which could upset these estimates. It is possible that after fifteen years, we may need a new airport if Dabolim cannot take the load and the Indian Navy does not relent. It is difficult to predict whether needs of the Navy would shrink or expand looking at the advances in technology. It is equally not easy to make future predictions of traffic i.e. beyond a fifteen year period due to the speed, quality and shift of advances in communications technology. Hence, it would make business sense if the matter of two airports was studied intensively since the demand and supply for airport facilities were well within the control and would stay so at least for another decade.

Undoubtedly, the Greenfield airport will work to absorb the entire traffic from Dabolim through fair, legal and normal business practices. Just a correspondence of assurances between the state and central government will not halt this process. The private airport operator will use all business tactics and promotions to kill the competitive location. Finally, Dabolim may bask in the glory of remaining an airport for VVIPs.

Section 4.

Politics of Identity & Status

> *The epicenter of this section is the identity issue. Goa which has successfully retained its distinct identity faces various challenges. The author has extensively discussed the various challenges and controversies disturbing the social harmony of Goa which includes the popular scripted perception that migrants are taking up local jobs and are threat to land, language and identity.*
>
> *Overall this section vastly covers the various aspects influencing out and in-migration and suggests a rational path to tackle the issue.*

Selling Impossible Dreams

Life in the hilly regions and areas of the North-Eastern States of India even after 75 years of Independent India would be a revolution and revelation for the population inhabiting the plains. These hilly tracts in British India were inhabited by tribal and aboriginal populations totally isolated from the mainstream of Indian society. They followed their traditional agricultural and social customs and their own animistic and tribal faiths. They were primitive, simple, unsophisticated, innocent and improvident. There was risk of their agricultural land passing to the civilised sections and the looming threat that these tribal populations may crawl into the clutches of the moneylenders.

Nothing much has changed with the special status provided under the Indian Constitution except two things. The Christian missionaries brought the "Ganga" of education and along with it clothed the tribal with a religion. The second is the Damocles sword of conflicts and bloodshed hovering all the time, making life and peace a casualty.

Great Wall of Protection

The problem of these backward areas was summed up in the Constituent Assembly formed to draft the Constitution for free India: "The areas inhabited by the tribes, whether in Assam or elsewhere are difficult to access, highly infested and lacking in civilizing facilities as roads, schools, dispensaries and water supply. The tribes themselves are for the most part extremely simple people who can be and are exploited with ease by plains folk........While a good number of superstitions and even harmful practices are prevalent among them, the tribes have their own customs and way of life with institutions like tribal and village panchayats or councils which are very effective in smoothing village administration. The sudden disruption of the tribals' customs and ways is capable of doing great harm. It is essential to provide statutory safeguards for the protection of the land which is the mainstay of the aboriginal's economic life and for his customs and institutions which, apart from being his own, contain elements of value".

The Report of the Sub-Committee on the Tribal and Excluded Areas of Assam (1947) documents the fear of exploitation by the people of the plains on account of their superior organisation and experience of business. Even if it is argued that the fear is unjustified, it has been the experience that land is usurped by people from the more advanced and crowded areas. In tribal areas, land is regarded as the property of the clan, including the forests. The Report also records that the hill people are extremely nervous of outsiders, particularly non-tribals. Hence, they value regulations like the requirement of an outsider to possess a pass to enter the hill territory beyond the Inner Line so that an undesirable person could be expelled.

It is against this backdrop that the Article 371 of the Indian Constitution strikes the balance between isolation and development. The objective was primarily directed to the preservation of social customs from sudden erosion and to safeguard the traditional vocations. This was to be supported by the second major objective of raising the educational level and standard of living. In the Constituent Assembly, Biswanath Das from Orissa was totally opposed to the whole concept of Scheduled Tribes and Scheduled Areas. He characterised this as nothing short of creating racial issues in the place of the communal issues which had resulted in the partition of the country. Munshi defended the object stating "We want the Scheduled Tribes in the whole country should be protected from the destructive impact of races possessing a higher and more aggressive culture and should be encouraged to develop their own autonomous life. They should not be isolated communities or little republics to be perpetuated for ever. Kuladhar Chaliha was critical of the proposals of the Drafting Committee and warned that the provisions of the Sixth Schedule giving considerable amount of autonomy to the district and regional councils would lead to the establishment of "Tribalistan" and the ultimate result would be "Communistan". Dr. Ambedkar reiterated that all safeguards have been provided in the constitutional framework to give inherent right to tribal people themselves and at the same time to ensure the authority of the State Legislature and the Parliament through process of consultation.

Groping in the dark

Earlier, there were feeble demands for special status for Goa. These weak voices were branded as the last residue of friends of Portugal or a section of Goans who are not comfortable with Indianisation of the land. This was the view held by groups claiming to be nationalists. A demand for application of special provisions of the Indian Constitution to Goa similar to those enunciated under Article 371 has been made by the Chief Minister of the State belonging to a political party which advertises "justice to all, appeasement of none". This could be the beginning of selling of an impossible dream to Goans. If Goans buy this project which can never reach completion, it is advantage for any incumbent in power at the State level. The agenda of election politics would be throwing put-shots at the Centre all the time.

I do not wish to say that there are no special aspects of Goa. There are in fact many things special about Goa which we do not find in the rest of the country. Goa did not have a single government-run primary school in the language of the land since 1961 till recently. Goans want their children to be educated through English-medium, not just from primary level but from nursery onwards. Majority of our MLAs take pride in taking the oath of office in any other language except the tongue of the soil. Hindus of Goa confidently believe that the language on their lips cannot be the language of their Gods and rituals. To cap it all, we have the history of the Opinion Poll and the struggle for recognition of Konkani by Goans themselves. Till date, we do not wish to affirm our language identity in one voice and all successive governments have been nervous on this front.

On a serious tone, let me say that trust was the traditional value wealth of Goa. Today, it's a desert of this value with no oasis insight. Post-statehood has made greed an inseparable ingredient in the diet of Goans. Goans are secular in mind, heart and worship. This pillar is infested with white-ants due to immigration and the inflow of religious capital from the rest of the country.

If we are looking at special treatment for drawing additional funds from the Central Government and additional funding for specific projects, it is possible through economic negotiation and political management. But, special status in terms of special provisions like the North-East would not be tenable.

Preserving Goa sans special status

> *If the government is committed to arrest alienation of lands and skewed demography, it is possible to a large extent even within the present framework. There is no need to wait for the luxury of the special status through a constitutional amendment.*

Are the intermittent and discontinuous showers of demand for special status for Goa the new opium sold to the peace-loving people of this tiny State? Or is it an alibi to cover our failures to safeguard the rights of the local populace to local resources including land within the existing framework of laws and the planning mechanism?

Special status is different from 'special category' states. As per the 13th Finance Commission, special category states are those with hilly terrain, sparsely populated, facing high transport costs resulting in high delivery cost of public services. The formula of central grants to loans for such states is in the ratio of 80:20 as opposed to 30:70 for others. Bihar and Orissa have made a demand to the centre for special category status in view of poverty, poor health indices, the size of population and the need for massive public works. This demand has not found favor with the centre in view of the enunciated criteria for special category states. The government of Goa has been making similar demands with the Planning Commission and related ministries arguing that the state joined the Indian Union fourteen years after independence and as a result missed the initial two-five year plans. I do not think that Goa can be accorded the special category status in terms of resource sharing from the central kitty. The indicators of per capita income, health, literacy and family planning are the best in the country. Goa is definitely facing public revenue limitations due to the diseconomies of small size but this is not a strong ground for special category status.

Special status for specially placed

We have constitutional guarantees in respect of special status under Articles 370 371, and 371A--371H of the Indian constitution. This is not to be viewed as a passport to separatism or erosion of national unity. Those who consider these provisions as an affront to Indian federalism have not understood the theory of "unequal" federalism wherein some states may enjoy a special status. The historical factors need special treatment for specially placed States. The special status is a strategy in a federal set up to satisfy the demand of national groups for political and cultural autonomy.

These provisions provide for constitution of Boards for Vidarbha, Marathwada, Saurashtra and Kutch. No Act of parliament in respect of ownership and transfer of land shall apply to Nagaland unless the Nagaland state assembly decides. The same holds true of religious, social practices of Nagas and the customary law and procedures. Similar clauses are extended to Manipur, Mizoram, Sikkim and Himachal Pradesh. Some of these states have enacted laws in respect of ownership of immovable property in their regions. In Mizoram, transfer of land by sale can take place within the members of the same tribe. Transfer of land holdings to non-tribes is prohibited by law in specified hilly areas to prevent alienation of land. A non-Mizo is given a restricted permit for stay and movement in Mizoram. As per the Himachal Pradesh land laws, transfer of land to non-agriculturist is barred. Non-agriculturist can only purchase land by the permission of the state government. Further, only permanent residents of Himachal Pradesh can buy land in the state. All others who wish to purchase land for projects are required to seek relaxations under the prevailing laws. Rules have been also relaxed in 2006 to allow non-Himachal residents to purchase land in certain specified areas. These are the examples of the possibilities of our federalism.

Perceptions graduate as realities

Mr. Shantaram Naik, Goa's MP in the Rajya Sabha spoke his mind to work for introduction of the bill in parliament to amend

Article 371(I) to authorize Goa state legislature for regulating ownership and transfer of land and also influx of immigrants. Today, the threat perception of alienation of land from the hands of locals including the community owned lands i.e. 'communidades' and the marginalization of the Goans looks to be a reality. It was in our hands to arrest this erosion and assert the purpose for which we gained statehood.

Much of our lands have been siphoned through government sponsored projects and schemes. Look at the working of the Goa Industrial Development Corporation and the disbursement of lands in the name of industrial development. The transfer of plots is most difficult for the locals and we have maintained a walk-in window for the non-locals. We were also thinking of similar vehicle to transfer more lands through the health estates and special economic zones. The new bug which will alienate the lands from the locals is the public-private partnership models worked out and implemented without transparency. The Goa Housing Board unsuitable and unacceptable design of tenements for locals is another case in point. This Board can teach how to convert beautiful areas into planned dirty and dingy slum-type localities.

Very Special People

Goans are very special people. We will talk of locals but give cent per cent priority to non-locals in terms of employment, award of public contracts, and sale of properties/real estate. We will lament at outsiders taking up our conventional occupations, trades, and enterprises in the service sector. However, we will not venture into such occupations or entrepreneurship.

We will ensure that our government locks the public resources in areas where the market/beneficiaries are prepared to finance. You can understand this from the rise in the number of English medium schools even at the pre-primary level. Goa is the only shining example of public grants to English medium schools at primary level. This cannot happen anywhere else in India, anywhere else in the world except maybe, where English is the mother-tongue. We know that the Konkani language is our identity but still we project Marathi also as our cultural identity. On the top of all this, we rationalize and justify the disconnect with Konkani even at the primary level. We believe in the superstition that English language is the key to future.

We bask in the glory of around six families democratically prepared to corner 45% of the seats in the Goa Assembly irrespective of the political party. We have made 'winnability' a corrupt and immoral process.

In Goa, everything is for sale and nothing seems to be impossible. The politicians are most accessible like a "tavern" on the roadside.

The question is whether Goa deserves a special status. It is a clear NO from my side. We are laid back people. The connect to Goa and its special identity is not visible beyond Internet and Facebook. It is the mass movement which needs to precede the special status. These are the lessons from Nagaland, Mizoram, Manipur and Telengana. If Goa is our homeland and we have to preserve this creation for generations, the status should not be gifted by New Delhi. We should be prepared to sweat and sacrifice.

If the government is committed to arrest alienation of lands and skewed demography, it is possible to a large extent even within the present framework. There is no need to wait for the luxury of the special status through a constitutional amendment.

Emigration of the Blue-Collared and Respectable

Remittances, which is money sent out home by people working away from home is an important and assured spring of foreign exchange. As per the World Bank Reports, India is the largest recipient of international remittances in the world. Around 35% of remittances originate from the Middle East and an equal share from North America. Europe accounts for 20% and the balance 10% from the rest of the world. This shows the concentration and spread of Indian emigrants. Despite being so, India cannot be regarded as a remittance-dependent economy as the remittance to Gross Domestic Product (GDP) ratio is just 4%. However, Kerala, Punjab and Goa are top remittance dependent economies as they account for 40% of international remittances. If these States are looked at as countries, they would figure as the top remittance-dependent nations of the world. This is only to highlight the mark of significance which needs to be accorded to the emigrant population and its impact on the growth prospects of the local economy. It is foolish to persecute them as lesser Indians as most of the nouveau nationalists tend to do today.

Goa has always been heavily dependent on this source. In the initial years post-liberation, it is the remittances which have shouldered the development of the State and sustained the economy. With subsistence agriculture and not so strong industry to generate any sort of economic take-off, it was mining and remittances which facilitated the local economic multiplier in trading, construction industry, real estate and an infant service sector. It is estimated that remittances to Goa from emigrants is around Rs. 850 crores per annum. This is approximately 6.3% of the State Gross Domestic Product and the quantum would be in the range of 30% of the revenue receipts of the Goa government.

This statistics should put a little wisdom in the minds of the local politicians who ridicule Goans for their propensity to migrate overseas. Goan Hindus tilting towards 'Hindutva' tend to make uncharacteristic comments on emigrating Goans even stretching it to questioning their patriotism on the ostensible belief that it is the local Christians and Muslims who dream to migrate. They need to know that youth from the Hindu community belonging largely to OBCs desire to take up even "disagreeable" overseas jobs to earn decent livelihoods for their families and also to create a security cover for their near future. The juicy pleasure that some politicians and armchair landlords pretending to be agriculturists take by poking fun at emigrants as rag pickers and toilet-cleaners is despicable. Today, it is skilled engineers, doctors, computer experts and professionals from the majority community who work their plans of education and employment across the borders.

The larger emigration is of the unskilled and the less literate. Around 78% of the emigrants have not crossed secondary education and the degree holders would be around 22%. It would be erroneous to describe this as brain drain as this human resource would be either unemployed or in some low paying seasonal jobs locally. Emigration creates shortage of local unskilled labour and shoots up the wage rate. Also, it results in "replacement migration" to fill the void. This partially explains immigration from neighbouring States into Goa taking up jobs and occupations which are considered 'undignified' but without which economic life cannot be in motion. As locals emigrate and out-migrate for reasons whatsoever, they need also to appreciate in-migration again for whatever motives. **It is really a contradiction that overseas Goans are the nastiest critics of migrants in Goa who later get assimilated into the region.**

Initially, emigrants will be drawn from specific communities. It would not be the equal urge of all to find income earning pastures overseas. It is normal to find minorities forming a larger proportion of emigrants. Their absorption levels under local environment in rewarding occupations are highly inadequate for reasons whatever. Their educational levels are also comparatively very low. These trends are bound to change with development providing equal access to all in education, health and employment. Hence, today we observe the propensity to emigrate across communities in Goa. The trends also indicate emigration of skilled, qualified and specialist human resource.

Remittances continue to finance the household consumption expenditure of sizeable population of the State. The non-resident Goans (NRG) remittance for family maintenance remains the primary purpose. The other slice gets channelized by NRG to domestic investments in real estate and share markets. The contribution of NRG to banks is quite substantial as foreign deposits constitute 22% of the total deposits in Goa. Remittance also funds charitable and religious institutions. The component in the form of gold and silver is also seen but negligible as compared to the cash component.

The uneven spread of migration from Goa is discernible from the inequality in the quality of life and consumption standards of the coastal regions and the hinterlands. This disparity is due to the remittance flow in the coastal belt which has provided boost to enlarged economic activity, apart from the areas being epicentres of tourism.

Apart from international migration, the national migration of the local population is also turning noticeable. The trend of the presence of the Goan community in the metros of India for exploiting opportunities is increasing. These drifts are inevitable in free and liberalized economic societies. This indicates that remittances, both international and internal would be crucial for Goa's growth and to sustain local investment, innovation and enterprise.

Migration: Escape from Poverty

International, intra-national, inter-state and intra-state migration is as old as the hills. Apart from the minor stimulus of novelty, adventure and quality of life, the major reasons for migration is to break the vicious circle of poverty, deprivation and the lack of opportunities. Despite the losses: of identity, of agreeable neighbourhood and of security in an unknown land, migration has proved to be the golden choice for people to find answer to unemployment, economic exploitation and unproductive life at home.

France, Germany, Canada, USA, Britain, Australia and the Gulf world have millions of migrants. Each one of this nation accounts for nearly 15% of foreign workers in their labour force. Millions of Indians have migrated to the rest of the world. It is estimated that Goans migration to other States of India and other parts of the world is around 25% of its population. The migration still and will continue. Immigration into this tiny State is also a regular phenomenon. Rough estimates suggest that migrants account for 20% of Goa's population.

Escape from equilibrium of joblessness

Migration is good for the families and children of those who migrate and those who remain behind. All those who move, better their position. They contribute to the economic development of the regions to which they migrate. They solve their personal problem of absolute poverty and also of those who remain at home since they turn productive and are no longer a burden on their home family as unproductive consumers. This is a natural remedy discovered by the poor without waiting for the government to implement alleviation programmes for them. Migration is a vehicle independent of the government to answer the problem of dispossession and denial of minimum levels of living.

Many including governments and planners look at migrants as guest workers. Locals consider them as trespassers and fit to be thrown out once their economic utility gets completed. This is due to poor understanding of facts and hence not a valid proposition. The migrants come with families and merge with the local population. As time matures, their children join schools, they become citizens, voters, adopt the language of the locals, participate in their cultural exchange, social fiestas and though initially face rejection, later get fully integrated with locals. At a later stage, their children and grand-children are not available for the same occupations for which the families migrated initially. Their children refuse to work at construction sites or in sweated factories or in municipal services. The economy needs the first generation unskilled and semi-skilled workers once again. After passage of time, these initial migrants look with suspicion and distrust the new migrants who enter as labour.

Stop migrants, halt development

It is true that migrants do not get the credit they rightfully deserve as economy boosters. Europeans do not hold the Asian workers in equal esteem. Even, President Barack Obama spoke unkindly about immigrants. They are painted as job thieves. 'Amchi Mumbai' fanatics terrorise the migrants from Hindi, Malayalam, Tamil, Telgu and Kannada speaking belts. Bengaluru locals cry hoarse "Only for Kannadigas". Goa also is a witness to such intermittent eruptions and more so during the election season.

This is because of our failure to see the larger picture. First of all, migration and immigration is inevitable. It can be considered as a need of development or a sin of underdevelopment. If we boot out migrants, the real estate and construction industry will definitely come to a grinding halt. Hotels, beach shacks and eateries will have to be closed. Factories would suffer. The same will be the situation in hospitals, nursing homes and municipal services. Fruits, vegetables, fish and essential goods would be in a sparse supply.

The contribution of the migrant population in terms of purchasing power along with the high propensity to consume also sustains self-employment, entrepreneurship and small business enterprise of the locals. This informal and unorganised economy will be in doldrums if the slice of the migrants is sucked from the population cake.

Migration has social and economic impact on home State and also the receiving State. There is a resource and brain drain from the home State. The skilled, trained and educated human power is solving the challenge of opportunities on their own through migration. In-migration is associated with pressures on land and civic amenities. There could be social and cultural stress due to influx.

Guns at migrants is perverseness

Let us understand the perceived costs of migration. What is clearly professed is social disturbance and conflict due to the threat perception to identity and culture. This should not be blown out of proportions because acculturation i.e. a change in the cultural behaviour through contact with another culture is also a happening event. Taking Goa as an example, the immigrants of the 80s and 90s would be the neo-Goans of the future. I am speaking of the work force which served the requirements of Goa. Their children have taken education in local institutions, made Goa as their home, learnt the local language and danced side by side to the cultural tunes with the local children of their age. Today, they are treated as "outsiders" in the State of their parent's birth.

The second threat perception is that the available employment opportunities are grabbed by migrants. This also needs to be examined against the facts. Employment is not fixed and a static concept. In fact, migration increases opportunities of employment and entrepreneurship. The third issue arises because of the pride of the home State since it is perceived that migration measures the failure of the State to take care of its people. There is also a guilt feeling amongst the migrants for having left the native land. This is natural and can be true if the decisions are not planned and voluntary.

People welcome international and interregional flights of capital and financial investment. However, with movement of human capital or resources we do not seem to be relaxed. The threat from capital which has captured Goa's coastline, land resources in the hinterlands and politics of the State would probably be irreparable. In our luxury to "live in the past" and pontificate about the "good old days", we label the migrants as vote banks, hunt them as outsiders and treat them as unwanted.

Migration in Goa: Gains and Concerns

> *"If Mumbai is cosmopolitan and a location to fulfill the dreams of all and sundry, it's because of migration. If Goa will not remain Goa, it's also a concomitant of migration and immigration".*

The story of migration and immigration will baffle a critical observer. It's a tale of contradictions. The flow of people 'inside' and 'outside' started from times immemorial and seems to have no end. Yet, migration is a disagreeable proposition for governments whether national or regional and looked at unkindly by local population. Though modern technology and communications is attempting to filter the world into a 'global village', national governments continue to be swayed by the theories of brain drain or gain. Concerns of national security, classifying people 'illegal', restricting citizenship and sprinkling salt of parochial national/regional pride are turning out to be priorities in the approach towards migration. The regional governments continue to weave the thread of 'sons of the soil' (Bhumiputra) and view migration as economic invasion and opportunities theft along with social pollution.

The story of migration is inseparable from the history of human civilization. The essence of migration or immigration is present in economic advancement, social development, technological breakthrough and assimilation of diverse cultures and lifestyles. **In short, let me submit that the three D's- Discovery, Development and Diversity is a function of migration.** Whether it is the architectural heritage that Goa boasts or the Goan cuisine appreciated the world over or the prestigious Silicon Valley in USA are all products impossible without migration. Yet, migration and immigration is not accepted with open arms.

In India, migration is around 30% with the inter-state and intra-state migration accounting for around 75% of the total migration. The international movement explains the balance. India is the largest remittance receiving country. Earlier, migration to a large extent was due to natural calamities, wars, communal riots and religious persecutions. The migration trend today is mainly due to opportunities of higher education, employment and better employment. For the poor and unskilled, their inter-regional and inter-state migration is largely to escape from poverty. The disadvantaged groups are driven by the "push factors" such as low income, low literacy and high poverty. The migration of the non-poor is to regions known for educational facilities and with strong presence of industry and service sector. It is the "pull factor" of high income and high literacy that draws the advantaged sections.

Migration is a truth of life. Movements such as 'Mumbai for Mumbaikars', 'Goem for Goemkars', 'Tamil Nadu for Tamils" could at most be regarded as temporary pain-killers. There seems to be no anti-dote for migration. Statistics reveals that migrant households are around 33 per thousand in urban areas and 13 per thousand in rural India.

- Do migrants take jobs and displace local workers or do they bring new skills in business and companies?
- Can we accuse migrants of business recession and cultural stagnation or do they bring the seeds of boom and vibrancy?
- Is it wrong to say that migrants harbor knowledge and take it from one location to another?
- Are not migrants' carriers of knowledge, skills, know-how, manual labor which can be further multiplied with the contribution of locals for gains to all?

Goans have been always migrating to metros in India and rest of the world. The dispersion of Goans is all around the globe. Goans are known the world over as a free and liberal community. Yet, locals largely hold migrants into Goa as dirty human beings, uncultured, pollutants, cause of all the ills and accuse them of stealing opportunities.

Goans migrating out of India are hunted as lesser nationals and mocked as owing allegiance to Western culture. This music from the self-professed nationalists belonging to the community of Hindus is to attack Goan Christians. Hindus conveniently forget that international migration from Kerala, Gujarat, Rajasthan is largely of Hindus. Somehow, inter-state migration is sought to be justified on grounds of inadequate opportunities locally.

A migrant is one whose current place of residence is different from the place of birth or the place of last residence. However, perception of locals is that "a migrant is always a migrant" and all the progeny born, educated and assimilated into local language, lifestyle and permanently settled in Goa are ridiculed as outsiders.

The immigrants-locals mix benefits all

- Colonial experience of 500 years making the chilli, cashew, tomato, potatoes, avocado and football intrinsically Goan with passage of time.
- Teachers from Kerala and Maharashtra contribution to school education and sports in Goa.
- Unskilled workers from the Border States of India building the infrastructure of Goa and facilities for growing urban population in Goa.
- The remittances of overseas Goans giving push to business and trading activity in Goa.
- Semi-skilled and skilled immigrants enabling the tourism and hospitality industry of the State.
- Nurses from Kerala complement the Health Industry of the State.
- The locals recombining the Chinese cuisine making it Goan Chinese.

- Goans in India and worldwide accounting for Brand Goa as a free, liberal, festive, trustworthy and cultured community
- The locals decorating the spices brought by immigrants creating the exclusive Goan prawn curry, vindaloo, cafreal, cooking masala on global space.
- 'Panipuri', and Chinese food joining the Ross Omlette and 'Cheris pao' on Goa's street food scene
- Western music and instruments woven with local and renovated as Goan music to the world
- Migration of Goans to metros contributing to education, life and careers of families.

Concerns, Conflicts and Contradictions

- *Perceived threat to job security of locals:*

Goans are averse to take up low and unskilled jobs. This is seen in all regions which have tasted rural economic security and affluence. Out-migration of Goans has created space for immigrants. The demands of infrastructure, tourism, fisheries, sweated industries, created the pull for immigrants. Their poverty levels and unemployment provided the push for their migration from hometowns. The locals find manual work disagreeable. They would be inclined if there is technology and human interface. This seems to be the **labour paradox** in Goa. There is unemployment of locals. At the same time, we have imported/migrant labour. Arun Sinha in his book Goa Indica has coined the phrase **"migrants in courtyard."** This is something which the locals detest. Migrant labour becomes the target due to the frustration of non-availability of agreeable avenues of employment.

- *Success of migrants in occupation and petty business*

The success of migrants in trading, para-engineering and technical services is not taken kindly by locals. This is also perceived as the dearth of entrepreneurial spirit of locals. To a large extent, this is a contributory factor for the verbal abuse in respect of migrants from N-E, Bihar, Orissa and Rajasthan.

- *Loss of control over the most scarce resource.. Land*

The land mafia and land bankers from the metros of India are taking control of this resource. Land and or real estate is put miles beyond the reach of locals. The real estate prices are unaffordable for the locals and the so termed 'outsiders' have invested either for speculative purposes or for a second home in Goa. This is not an offshoot of migration per se as these investors and speculators are not productively locked in the state. This is an issue which needs to be answered through effective legislation.

- *Threats to identity*

Raj Thackarey repeatedly says "When I open my door, I see a Bihari working outside". The Goans lament that all the languages except the local Konkani are the sounds in the market. The perception of threat to the "uniqueness" of Goa is gaining ground.

What is this uniqueness?

The observation of Shyam Benegal who shot "Trikaal" and "Bhumika" in Goa is pertinent here. To quote ""At first sight, Goa does not seem too different from its coastal neighbours, Maharashtra in the North and Karnataka in the South. Soon enough, you notice that Goa is well distinctly Goan." Raunak Singh, Chairman of the Committee on site for Free Port had the following to say about Goa. "The other contenders have all that Goa has and perhaps more, but they don't have Goa".

A negative angle about Goa is that it is also depicted as a location where one will die of boredom. This is hitting at the laid back attitude of the locals. The other positive angle is that Goa is a location to slow down giving you time to do many things you want to do. This is drawing writers, artistes and creative minds to settle in Goa as the natural and human environment is conducive for intellectual stimulation.

Immigration and particularly of the poor and disadvantaged sections has multiplied the issues of housing, cleanliness and sanitation. There are pressures on public amenities and primary health care. This calls for an effective implementation of the provisions of the Interstate Migrant Workmen Act, 1979.

Though Goans migrating overseas is bringing in remittances and providing better employment there are issues at home. Children of migrant Goans growing up in Goa is a sensitive subject as adolescence is a turbulent period. The absence of parents at home, easy money and access to gadgets have thrown up psychological questions and motivational issues for learning in early years. For children left behind, the parental migration is challenging. Migration of Goans has brought opportunities, it has also created insecurities. Of late, the migration overseas and to the rest of India has raised issues of aged parents left behind and loss of connection with children and grandchildren. This has also accentuated the sale and release of ancestral properties to developers.

Despite the growing concerns, it is submitted that restricting immigration and migration would be bottlenecks on the extension of knowledge and skills. Countries and States which are open to migrants will prosper faster. This is truer in respect of skilled migration. In today's modern times, we should dethrone the Brain Drain theory and evolve the Global Gain approach. The Son of the Soil or Bhumiputra approaches within States in a nation would restrict national gain.

The Changing Demography of Goa

(with inputs from Akbar Gaded)

> *Migrants have made Goa their home; they are the 'nouveau Goans' with their children completing their education in local schools and colleges.*

On May 30, 1987 Goa became the 25th State of the Indian Union. This Konkani speaking region commemorates 37 years of statehood. An independent State as opposed to a territory under administration of the central government was a reasonable and genuine aspiration of Goans under the backdrop of Goa's distinct language, lifestyle and identity.

There are a few who feel that Goa lost the public revenue advantage and central government funding arrangements of the union territory days. They hold a considered view that considering the small size of the territory and limited economic options, it would have been wiser to delay the grant of statehood by at least a decade so as to enable completion of major infrastructure projects through central funding. It's true that Goa is handicapped in terms of raising its own public revenue of the proportions required for development projects and to support social security schemes. However, that's not an unfair price to be paid for the statehood status as along with this flows greater political autonomy and independence. Revenue generation for public projects would remain a constraint and a challenge for this tiny region. The State needs cost consciousness, public expenditure discipline and rationalization of freebies from public exchequer Effective tax collection through better tax administration and plugging of leakages can provide substantial revenue without tinkering with the rates and tariffs. The government could evolve private-public partnerships in infrastructure projects to answer the revenue challenge.

Thirty-seven years down the line, it looks that Goa along with development has also integrated with the unhealthy currents of the national mainstream. Political and bureaucratic corruption has become an acceptable way of life. The proverbial social harmony of this envious slice of India is under attack with seeds of communal discord and mistrust getting fertilized and receiving political patronage.

Goa and Goans need to navigate successfully three critical issues at this juncture. A shadow of negativity seems to have gripped Goans. We seem to be masters to oppose and develop cold feet to propose alternatives. The anti-migrant sentiment, derogatory references to migrant workers and the social media flogging and whipping of non- locals defeats the essence of Goa and Goenkarponn (Goaness). Goans will have to make deliberate efforts to preserve the social harmony which is currently under trial and conserve its unique natural environment which is put on sale under pretext of economic development by greedy politicians and vested business interests.

The demography of Goa has changed and the same is noticeable in towns and villages. Migrants in search of occupation, employment, trade and business have made Goa their home over the years. They are the 'nouveau Goans' with their children completing their education in local's schools and colleges. Konkani is on their lips and Goa has become their land of birth. They are in public employment, private sector or as professionals and self-employed. They are as locals as anybody professing to be local on the ground of birth. This needs to be underlined as their first home, not a second home like those of the affluent and privileged falling in the big, bold and beautiful category. Added to this there is a huge chunk of floating migrants in Goa. These groups were held hostage by the pandemic. They are unwanted at workplace and unwelcome at their native place being guided under COVID19 protocol and SOPs. They were devastated by the lockdown. Their families craved for their presence at their native place.

Talking of Goa as 'motherland' and holding the cudgels to fight for "existence of Goans in their own land" topping it up with anti-migrant sentiments continues to be easy road to politics and social power. Such romanticism has persuasive influence over the gullible natives and builds the emotional connect with people of Goan origin worldwide. Such groups tend to make migrants scapegoats for every crisis-----unemployment, dirt, disease, pollution, crime and democratic outcomes. The pandemic resulted in the exodus of migrant population out of the State. This automatically created empty space on the contractual employment disc.

The turmoil inflicted by the pandemic is also resulted in a reverse migration of Goans back home. Goa experienced acute labour shortages as the locals find such engagements and callings "disagreeable". The pandemic fall out should cease the flogging of productive migrants and putting them on the guillotine. The easy road of grabbing political eyeballs and eventual leadership by abusing the migrant card should be put on pause. Inducements by providing that 'labor gets its due' in terms of wages and social security could open the field for locals. At present, the industry pays the workers as per the 'labor standards' which are abysmally low as it is their poverty that drives labor to accept unfair wages and terms of contract. The very fact that migrant workers are available at call only testifies the abject poverty and absence of subsistence employment in their native lands. As things returned to normal, migrants returned to fill the empty spaces on the contract employment disc.

Goa is perceived to be safe and its smallness provides the access to public services with least strain. This motivates many migrant families to settle down in this region.

The Race for Portuguese Nationality

Around four members of Village Panchayats in Goa have been disqualified as they were ineligible to contest elections to political institutions as not being citizen of India. They are holding a Portuguese passport, meaning thereby that by law and their conduct, they had acquired Portuguese citizenship. There are unconfirmed reports of the possibility of MLAs holding similar travel documents. It would not be an exaggeration to hold that around twelve thousand Goans may be actually residing in Goa who have been either allotted or who have reached the final stages of receiving what they consider as the prized document. There is credence to these figures since the number of Goans who have applied for surrender of Indian passport to the Regional Passport Office; Goa (RPO) for the period 2006 to June, 2012 is nearing 9600. It is revealed that on an average 20 Goans per day submit their applications for surrender certificate to RPO, Goa. The surrender certificate of Indian Passport is issued by this office after obtaining the no-objection from Ministry of External Affairs, New Delhi. Such a surrender or renunciation certificate needs to be produced at the time of applying for Portuguese passport. There are many who do not hold an Indian passport and hence can apply directly for a Portuguese passport. However, there are few who hide the factual details and hold Indian as well as Portuguese passport. Goans from all communities, working beyond the shores of India or having strong intention to work overseas and the lust of eventually settling outside India forms the potential demand force for Portuguese passport. A Portuguese citizenship means a safe, smooth and hassle-free passage to Europe.

Hum Aapke Hai Kaun

What is special in our relationship with Portugal that makes things simple and easy for Goans to move to Europe? On what grounds does Portugal entertain applications to grant Portuguese nationality?

It is nothing else but the accident of history i.e. the colonisation and the liberation of Goa. Goans born prior to 19th December, 1961 though of Portuguese nationality by birth automatically became Indian citizens by the Goa, Daman & Diu Citizenship Order, 1962. This resulted in a unique situation wherein people of Portuguese nationality acquired new citizenship. All those born prior to liberation had their birth registered with the "Conservatoria dos Registos" (Registry) in Goa and this registration meant provision of the birth-certificate which was known as "Certidade de Nacimento". This is nothing more than certificate of birth. Almost all Goans born in Portuguese Goa would have such a document of birth.

The Portuguese government entertains applications from any of its citizens from the erstwhile colonies for grant of what is called as "Billet de Identidade" (National identity card). This is applicable for all Goans born prior to liberation or for those who are born post-1961, if one of the parents was born in Portuguese Goa (prior 1961) and their birth and marriage are registered in Lisbon. The first step to apply for Portuguese passport is to get the birth and marriage of parents registered in Lisbon. It is only after these records are entered and maintained at the Registry in Lisbon, the next stage i.e. application for the Portuguese passport commences. Registration of birth entitles the person to apply for nationality by birth. This means that mere registration of birth would not make a person a Portuguese citizen. So, after registration of birth, if the person applies for "Billet de Identidade" i.e. gives the consent or uses this instrument as a travel document and passport, it would mean that the person has given up Indian citizenship and acquired Portuguese citizenship.

Having given up Indian citizenship, the stay of such a person in Goa is permissible only on application and grant of a residence visa. Such a person would have to also abide by the provisions of the Foreigners Registration Act. At the same time, a mere registration of birth i.e. citizens card in Portugal (cartao de cidadao) would not invite any infirmity or disqualification.

To be or not to be

India does not recognise dual citizenship. However, considering the special privilege that Goans are accorded by Portugal, if given the opportunity of dual citizenship, Goans would be eager to grab. In fact, a demand for dual citizenship is emanating from overseas Goans and Indians who have acquired foreign citizenship. This demand is being argued on grounds of facilitating investment and contribution to economic and social development of the land of birth. The trend amongst Goans to acquire Portuguese citizenship/passport is largely because of the possibilities of opportunities of employment and settlement. A few opt for it because they perceive better quality of life in Europe and a few others carry a negative complex of their land. I am quite sure that the positive trend for Portuguese passport is for self-interest and private gains. It has nothing to do with love for Portugal or anti-Indian sentiment or feeling. Hence, let us not read factors like nationalism and patriotism into this trend.

With the possible spectre of over twelve thousand Goans residing in Goa with Portuguese nationality and or passport documents, the Government of Goa; the Ministry of External Affairs, Govt. of India; the Foreigners Registration Office of Goa Police have to demand information and transparency from the Portuguese Embassy and Consulate. One is free to acquire any citizenship. At the same time the laws of the land should be followed. Under the veil of secrecy and friendly relations with foreign governments, the government of India and the government of Goa should not make matters so difficult for itself and other citizens that Goans opting for Portuguese nationality adorn the seats in our legislatures, local-governing bodies and other instrumentalities of the government with gay abandon. The powerless individual citizens are expected to lead documentary evidence with government and the judiciary to prove the renunciation of Indian nationality by acquiring the

Portuguese passport. Considering the magnitude of the issue at hand, the State and Central Government and also the higher judiciary should not wash off the hands and continue with a totally helpless posture.

Making People Illegal

The Constitution of India puts no restraints on free mobility of citizens within the country. However, the threat perception of locals to regional identity and loss of opportunities of business and employment is fomenting anti-migrant sentiment in many states of India. Tendencies to paint migrants as responsible for crime and making daily life unsafe are gaining support from locals. It is well known that poor and underprivileged migrants are engaged in 'disagreeable', sweated, and unskilled activities. Yet, they are hunted for the dirt and unhygienic conditions. Little we appreciate that without migrant labour, our cities would be paradise of dirt, filth, disease and squalor. The public infrastructure projects would come to a grinding halt.

Holding that the loyalty of the migrants is to their native region and state of origin, a furore is created when migrants line up for electoral card. Actually, the fundamental right to migrate in any part of the country is ineffective without the right to vote. Any citizen who has been living in a place for more than six months can apply for registration as a voter, if not already registered. If registered, the person can apply for revision to the new place of residence. It is immaterial whether a person lives in shed or pavement or without any roof. Locals eye with suspicion and oscillate with venom when migrants are allotted Aadhar, ration card or any other such document to avail public utilities and services. These prejudices are present not only in small states like Goa but also in bigger states like Maharashtra, Karnataka, Andhra Pradesh, Gujarat and Assam.

This 'outsider' doctrine of treating the otherwise 'insiders', all being Indian citizens has no legal and constitutional approval. Even otherwise, it should not gather roots in a civilized and humane society. Political parties, particularly regional outfits and politicians who are self-anointed torch-bearers of nationalism and patriotism surprisingly cling to this doctrine to appease the regional voters. At the same time, they would feign concern for the plight of migrants. What was despicable was a Goa Minister known for dancing with migrants suddenly declaring a public policy of providing toilets through public funds only for locals and not for migrants. Chauvinist groups in Karnataka make the life of skilled migrants uncomfortable in their state. Politicians' game seems to be to keep the migrants in a trauma of being illegal 'citizens' in their region state and they step in as protectors.

Refugee, human trafficking, contract labour and migration----- all have origins in poverty and displacement due to man-made and natural calamities. If this is properly assimilated then we will not allow the absurdity that is going on in Assam under the National Register of Citizens (NRC). No doubt, it is a fall out of the Assam Accord signed by Rajiv Gandhi in 1985. This was to broker peace with the leaders of the Assam movement demanding identification and deportation of illegal immigrants. The NRC updation as mandated by the Supreme Court in 2013 has resulted in the government cuffing up 1300 crore by engaging 40,000 government employees. This winnowing has identified around 19 lakh illegal immigrants from 3.29 crore applicants. They are unable to produce a satisfactory document that their parents or grandparents were Indian citizens. Almost all the so termed "illegal" people have spent over four decades scaling the mountainous terrain and swimming in the rivers and waterways. There are quite a number of Biharis, Bengalis, Gorkhas and Assamese left out of NRC. This is the story of the lesser known, unknown and unorganized people.

From the known, the people not counted are shocking. A 72 year old retired school teacher. A 62 year old Assam MLA. The names of kin of former President Fakhruddin Ali Ahmed were missing. These are not stray instances. Initially, 40 lakh were counted as illegal immigrants. It's now 19 lakh after rounds of screening for multiple years. It has been turmoil for people and families with no tangible result for the state or nation. It is the aged, women and children who are under stress and in jails or detention camps. People have spent their time and money for documentation making rounds after rounds to the tribunals.

Most of those, out of the list cannot be expected to appeal to High Court or Supreme Court considering their economic condition and access to appeal.

The worse is yet to come. The Chief Minister of UP wants to implement NRC in his state. The Delhi unit chief of BJP is demanding NRC for Delhi. The Haryana CM says "We will implement NRC". The Sangh eyes NRC to target Muslims all over India. There is a renewed demand for NRC in Christian dominated Meghalaya, Mizoram and Manipur. A Citizenship Amendment Bill seeks to make illegal migrants who are Hindus, Sikhs, Buddhists, Jains, Parsis and Christians from Afghanistan, Bangladesh and Pakistan, eligible for citizenship. The Muslims are excluded probably sending the message that they have no place in India. Religion laced citizenship would be yet another cruel onslaught on the Indian Constitution.

NRC offers no positive benefits to the country. As per 2018 data of Ministry of External Affairs, the number of Indian NRIs and PIOs is 310 lakh. We all revel in the contribution and achievements of overseas Indians. Can we not close the NRC chapter to provide security and end the agony of our people? After over forty years, they are ours, aren't they?

Migrants are Assets, not Criminals

The Chief Minister's verbal frown on the floor of the Goa Assembly blaming migrant workers for the increasing crime rate in Goa would on one side embolden the anti-migrant sentiment and on the other side provide relief to the police and law enforcing agencies as they have a saleable reason to explain their failures. Crime statistics would most likely disprove such beliefs. It is possible that there are criminal elements amongst the immigrants as we have within the locals. Just as workers, executives and traders immigrate; the criminals use the same road and railway routes. However, this constitutes a microscopic fraction. The majority of migrants are performing productive economic activities; otherwise they just cannot survive in the immigrated land.

Migration is unstoppable

I am not making either a case for migrants or against them. The reality is that migration and immigration has come to stay. It is unstoppable and inevitable. Initially, the backward and disadvantaged groups are characterised by high rates of geographical mobility i.e. migration. Poverty, unemployment and the shift from agriculture are the earlier indicators. However, migration of professional and technical population along with affluent executives is associated with the march of the economy from industrialism to service sector. The earlier is the drain of labour from neighbouring states to Goa and later could be described as the brain drain from Goa to the rest of India and overseas. Goa is a subject of both at one and the same time.

Goa being a small state with a cosmopolitan culture and yet a unique identity, migrants are viewed as those who disturb this exclusive balance. In relation to the geographical and demographic compass of other states of India, Goa is different. There are social, cultural and identity issues at stake, more particularly in the coastal villages. Today, we find an equal number of migrants in the village bazar as the locals. It is this threat of skewed numbers that foments the anti-migrant emotion. It is against this background that we notice the Gram Sabhas and Village groups of Goa opposing almost all proposals of investment or development in the village. To a large extent, the opposition at the Gram Sabha is from those members who are defeated at the Panchayat elections. With a multi-cornered contest at Panchayat elections, the aggregate number of defeated candidates is sizeable in relation to the elected members of the Panchayat. It is really a funny situation wherein the elected Panchayat is held hostage by the Gram Sabha under the domineering influence of the candidates who are rejected by the village electorate and who later form the active component at the Gram Sabha. In the Gram Sabha, we hardly find 'propositions'.

Goa would not be a land of opportunities as it is today subtracting the contribution of migrants which is our target of attack. We see their involvement in all the sectors filling the void created by non-availability of local human power. Real estate, housing, public works and infrastructure projects would not move ahead without migrant labour. There is wide presence of migrant workers in resorts, hotels and shacks which constitute the tourism sector. Extractive industries such as mining and industries vulnerable to high pollution depend on outside labour. Migrants take the share as traders in fish, vegetable and fruit markets. Water supply, irrigation, gas pipe line, major and minor bridges and sewerage projects could be commissioned due to the sweat of the migrants.

Workers not criminals

We need to acknowledge that migrant workers come from their villages to almost a homeless existence either in towns or neighbouring states. The motivation is to earn a passport for vertical mobility and a different life for their children. They come with this hope in towns and cities and initially are forced to work in almost inhuman and insanitary conditions. They work on public projects wherein the government contractors do not adhere to any norms of labour laws and social security. Many of them climb on the ladder as small entrepreneurs and traders. Some are fortunate to provide education to their children to enable them to take up skilled occupations.

Positioning migrant workers as criminals may serve the appetite of locals who regard such workers as nuisance. We need to understand that migrant workers are an unavoidable concomitant of the development process and the prevalent social structure in our country. We should not allow the parties, police and enforcement agencies to wash off their hands by gumming the label of criminal on the migrant workforce.

Migrants are people not demons

Come elections to the state legislatures or the local self-governing bodies, the politicians pound the anti-migrant drums sowing seeds of mistrust and raising the bogey of local interests and identity. The guns are largely aimed at the poor and marginalized groups. It is a stoic silence when it comes to investors in industrial properties, speculators in agricultural and beach properties and consultants in public projects. If the genuine concern is of illegalities, the focus should be on blunders and misdemeanours whether of migrants or natives. Getting intoxicated with the anti-migrant alcohol can only provide a false high to the native population and an easy alibi to gloat in the failures by putting a cover on the realities. It is only the positive harnessing of the energies of all that will ensure the economic growth of the state and retain Goa as the region of liberalism, inclusiveness and social harmony.

Domestic migration is around 30% in India on an average. There is seasonal exodus of labour from poverty stricken and drought prone pockets to areas which require unskilled and sweated labour particularly in sectors such as fisheries, mining, construction, plantations and infrastructure. The initial migrants who get stabilized in the migrating state would later choose the options of trade, business, professions and better employment. The GenNext of the intital migrants gets assimilated into the lifestyle, language and culture of the locals and vice-versa. This is a concomitant of development and a continuous process with no exceptions found to the contrary. What explains immigration into Goa also elucidates domestic and international emigration of Goans. This evolution is unstoppable, though there could be public policies to provide preferential treatment to local and natives in specific sectors. However, *"a successful war against migrants is impossibility, treating the flock as enemy is suicidal and holding them in contempt is dehumanizing."*

Anti-migrant fights wherein the migrants are heckled and prevented from carrying on their trade is definitely not a welcome sign for the state. It is a misguided route adopted to ostensibly protect the interests of the locals in certain traditional trades. Social media is rife with news of Goa turning unsafe due to migrants. Many 'insiders' paint the 'outsiders' as corrupt, criminals and looters. It is wrong to assume that the state will be free from crime, corruption and burglary if the migrant population is ejected from the territory. A new breed of youth leaders are fishing for political and social space by fomenting anti-migrant sentiments under the guise of guarding regional identity and economic interests of natives. This track will multiply conflict and social tension rather than attempt to solve the problems of the people. If stretched to extremes, it could be a potential source of negative backlash against the emigrants from Goa. We are inviting flare-ups against Goans with such narrow vision and impractical approach to migrant population.

It is true that the migrant population is sharing space with locals in petty trades and business. This is largely visible in the vegetable and fruit markets all over the state. Most of these migrants have become permanent settlers with their children enrolled in schools, colleges and university and the families availing public services just as the native population. Their second generation has made entry into professions, small and medium businesses and government services. Some specific traditional occupations which are considered as forte of natives such as bakery, fish trade and retail trade has invited increased participation of the migrant settlers with locals phasing out for other lucrative and agreeable alternatives. The migrant settlers are providing the required utility services to household sector in the state and exploiting the opportunities wherever there is a vacuum.

Intermittent tensions due to clash of economic interests are understandable and they should be dealt with in business-like fashion rather than singling out competitors for abuse because they happen to be migrants. Such pressures are seen even within locals. There have been instances in the distant past when the traders housed in a Municipal market in South Goa town were up in arms with traders in a newly sprung location christened as the 'Gandhi market' holding that in this marketplace there are all sorts of illegalities. Today, the traders from the 'Gandhi' market are enraged over locals from neighbouring talukas selling the agricultural produce in the town and are quick to declare this trade as illegal. If these are appreciated as economic conflicts rather than giving the colour of locals versus migrants and locals versus Scheduled Tribes and solved in harmonious manner by taking all on board, it would be gain to all and to the state.

"Whether it is inter-state or intra-state migration or international migration, the critical issue is economic. The yearning for identity will continue but it is a shadow and stays elusive." It is the economic cake which spurs migration and the anti-migration sentiment is due to the increased competition to share the economic cake. At the same time, migration also fuels demand in the economy creating possibilities of expanding the size of the market. Without in-migration, Goa and the villages may outwardly look serene and peaceful. However, the Goan economy and more particularly the village economy would be in doldrums also taking into account the out-migration. We hardly question the local trappings of a non-resident Goan or a person of Goan origin who looks at Goa as a purely holiday destination or an emotional connect through the distance mode. We tend to attack and abuse those who have made Goa their home.

Goans and Migrants: A Changing Discourse.

(With inputs from Akbar Gaded)

Goa, a pulchritudinous land of history, secular culture and leisure destination has evolved socially, politically and economically into a strong civilized state prosperously retaining its unique identity, language and culture. This has fascinated many descendants of Adam to explore their interest in it. Every year thousands of humans set their journey towards Goa, some for leisure while many to explore their economic fantasies of which the government has no record, supervision or control. The expeditious industrialization and urbanization in the state paved a way for Independent Indian citizens who did not hesitate to race along with Goans to grab the convenient economic opportunities, resulting into a slow and steady migrant settlement which was not realised until it was politically epitomised and bombarded on Natives by some bellwethers waiting for their political expanse. Thus, regionalism began to spread its wings among the Goan masses engendering a divide between the native Goans and the migrant settlers. It is estimated that 35% of Goa's population constitutes migrants who are withal believed to be the root cause of unemployment and increase of crime rate in Goa.

Today the conspicuous percentage of migrants haunts Goans over their culture and identity and this has led to the spread of the anti-migrant propaganda irately in Goa asserting migrants have surmounted employment opportunities of natives and incriminating them of all the criminal and illegal activities budding up in Goa.

Prompted by the sedative influence of exorbitant regionalism, local individuals as well as self-acclaimed activist groups, are out on a reconnaissance with their Smartphone's reporting and exposing alleged illegal shanties, businesses and the obscure nexus between the migrants and the ruling government over the social media platforms. Though the investigation by locals has exposed few illegalities but it has created an anarchic situation where the poor migrant vendors fall prey to harassment, insults and abuse by locals. The anti-migrant propaganda has withal invigorated a hunt to identify the aboriginals (original Goans) straining out the migrants (settlers).

There is an unequivocal echo heard across Goa to deport all the migrants back to their respective states which they believe is the only solution to all socio-economic and political problems.

The organised regional hysteria among the innocent natives may have orchestrated the inculpation towards the settled community of migrants but the picture isn't what it looks like. A higher probe is needed on the matter to its utmost depths since the lead direction will engender many rifts in the secular Goan society and inter-state relations which every Goan must acknowledge and reflect upon.

Metamorphosis of Anti-Migrant Sentiment:

The ascension of regionalism resulted in an auspicious advantage for the minorities, protecting their culture, language and identity but it is often misused to divide the community, engender vote banks and to achieve political mileage. The case of Goa is no different since the regional sentiments are often rejuvenated as obliged by the leaders. Every mandate and the rudimentary approach is to inject fear and suspicion among natives against migrant settlers proclaiming migrants will soon surpass the native population leading to ethnic dilution.

There is no authentic data outlining the exact number of migrants in Goa but the figures are often soothsaid and misquoted to instil fear among natives under the pretext of preserving regional identity.

No doubt Goa as an economic fantasy land magnetized a cumbersomely hefty influx of migrants who underwent the process of social mobility to intermingle with Goan community by emulating Goan lifestyle but they are still quantified as outsiders and a threat to Goan distinctiveness and ethos. Even the Chief

Minister of Goa, Mr Pramod Sawant expressed his solicitousness over rampant migration in Goa and stated: *"Migrants would soon outnumber the indigenous population" (News18, 2019).*

The migrants who were earlier yanked from the neighbouring states for the required labour have now become a pop in the eye just because they opt to settle in Goa. Evoking the migrant settlements as a threat to Goan identity and culture, the incipient toddlers zealous for a political vocation has gained applaudable success across Goa by promoting anti-migrant sentiments. The social media platforms are flooded with news and videos of the migrant vendors who are driven out from their spot of business, harassed and admonished by locals to go back to their respective states. There are number of WhatsApp and Facebook groups promoting abhorrence against migrants.

The endorsed anti-migrant propaganda momentarily hovering across Goa was an outcome of an event when a man from the Lamani community (Nomadic Tribe) got a taxi permit to ply his vehicle at Benaulim village. Natives immediately reacted arguing that the taxi business is a traditional business of natives and no outsider shall be sanctioned to enter on the traditional business turf. The rage was further intensified when local newspapers were inundated with 'Name' and 'Surname' change advertisements by migrants who were adopting Goan local 'Names' and 'Surnames' thoroughly transmuting their identity. The transmutation of 'Name' and 'Surnames' like *Ramchandra Birappa Hirukade to Ramchandra Birappa Mayekar, Ramesh Lamani to Ramesh Naik, Mallappa Masmardi to Mark Mascarenhas, Mohan Karunakaran to Jimmy Lobo, Mehrunissa Charangan to Alice Rodrigues, Raja Benkappa to Raja Damian Almeida, Ponnuswamy Marianathan to Mario Nathan* etc. raised a number of doubts.

Change of 'Surnames' makes a great deal in Goa because of mundane ethos that there are certain native 'Surnames' which have very high leverage with which one can relate or ostensibly authenticate his/ her identity as native Goan. These native

'Surnames' have been utilized by migrants allegedly to veil their identity, to grab properties of landowners with no heir, to get caste certificates, to get Portuguese passport and citizenship, to obtain welfare schemes and to get Government jobs. One of such case was reported in Benaulim village, a tenant in the house of an elderly couple made them her legal parents without their cognizance and then obtained a birth certificate, driving license, registered her marriage and applied for Portuguese Passport. Dreaded by such disquieting events, natives have developed detestation which is fuelled further by the zealous bellwethers appeasing the natives for political gain portraying migrants as the scapegoat for all the crises faced by the natives.

The high rate of unemployment among the youths of Goa is also surmised to be the product of established monopoly of migrants over local business opportunities.

Majority of the Goans believe that because of migrants, natives lose job opportunities in Goa.

Today, almost 60-70% space is allegedly occupied by migrants, whether be it Mapusa market, Panaji market, Ponda market, Sanquelim market, Calangute market, Banastari market, Vasco market or any other market. Migrants have gained a monopoly over local businesses like fish, meat, vegetables, flowers and other utilities. Migrants are additionally found selling snacks like Bhel Puri, Ros Omelette and light refershment across streets. It is rumoured that migrants have developed a syndicated network dominating every sector, more espacilly grocery and hardware. Natives also incriminate the politicians for supporting and backing the migrants.

The Demagoguery approach of anti-migrant dilemma has contaminated the rational competency of innocent Goans who are living under the veil of ignorance.

The tussle of "Identity" between a Goan and a non-Goan has led to the ascension of regional jingoism. "Who is a Goan and a Non-Goan?". The answer to this is not easy but a marvel of intricacies.

In the midst of this turmoil the Revolutionary Goans Party(RGP) supposedly pledged to protect the Goan culture, identity and land has come up with their definition of a Goan which is also the crux of a reverie antidote kenned as the POGO (Person of Goan Origin). The POGO defines *"A person of Goan Origins is a person who is or whose parents or grandparents, or either one of the parents or grandparents was born in Goa prior to 20 December 1961 or who had a permanent habitation in Goa prior to 20 December 1961 and is also a citizen of India. (All descendants of a person including a minor) of Goan origin shall be person/s of Goan origin provided they are citizens of India":* rest all shall be deemed as migrants and shall not be given any privilege or to take part in the process of governance, owning land, employment etc.

It further states, if a question arises as to whether any person is of Goan origin or not, then the Collectors of the respective district of North and South Goa shall decide such issues after discerning the parties and grant a certificate to the effect that person is of Goan origin. Any erroneous information provided to the Collector by any party applying for the certificate shall be deemed to be a cognizable offence and the same will have a simple confinement for a period of 1 year and a fine of Rs. 5 lakhs.

Occupied by regional demagoguery, it is no wonder why after 62 years of liberation a desideratum was felt to identify the original Goans.

There are few who hold that the only indigenous people of Goa were Kunbis, Gaudas, Velips and Kharwis; the former three engaged in agriculture while the Kharwis engaged in fishing occupation.

Prof. Dr Olivinho J. F. Gomes in his book "A Concise History of Goa" states that the original Goans belonged to Proto-Australoids or Austrics (Adivasis) and their scions today in Goa are kenned as Gauda, Kunbi, Velips, Dhangar and Mhar who were latter dispossessed of their ancestral lands by the Dravidians and the Indo-Aryans.

Mr Joao Antonio Jacinto da Costa also substantiates the original inhabitants of Goa were Gaudas, Kunbis, Mahars.

Goa was then ruled by many dynasties like The Mauryas, The Bhoj, The Chalukyas, The Shilahars, The Kadambas, The Mughals and The Portuguese. They all gave their unique culture, tradition, cuisine and essence which shaped and gave a secular resplendence to Goa.

It is now understood by following the traces of History, which lays substantial evidence that the aboriginal community of Goa are the Gauda, Kunbi, Velips and Kharwis and rest all were migrants who later settled and established their hegemony.

Identifying as Goans to only those who have family lineage up to 1961 is a nebulous notion. One needs to turn the pages of the history of Inquisition period which records the out-migration of many Goans who fled to the parts of Karnataka like Kumta, Karwar, Ankola, Udupi, Mangalore, Sirsi, Bhatkal and parts of Maharashtra like Malvan, Sawantwadi, Vengurla, to save themselves from conversion and to save their Kuldevtas. It is a vague adventure to prove or to ask the authenticity of being a Goan because there is no such thing. The state of Goa is shaped by the migrants and it still perpetuates with new migrants today.

According to the State domicile Act "a person who holds 15 years domicile certificate is considered as a Goan". Setting a line or a date to authenticate a Goan is an imprudent dilemma.

- *Goan Name and Surnames- Decoding the myth*

The mediocre mindset of Indians still considers some Titles, Names and Surnames as very consequential and meritorious. In Goa, there are few alleged prevalent Names and Surnames which have good leverage and through it, Goans endeavour to identify a Goan and a Non-Goans.

Many self-acclaimed activists are found interrogating the migrant vendors and the first question they ask is ***"Tera Naam*** *kya hai?"* if he states *"Sanjay Tiwari"* then the immediate reaction is *"Tiwari Goa ka Naam hai kya?" "Tu kidar ka hai?" "Tere gaav me jake business Kar Goa me kyu aata hai?" "Goa ka Naam kharab kiya tum logo ne"* etc. This depicts the racist mentality of innocent Goans who have been sedated with the negative essence of regionalism. There are many Goans who still judge and exibite pride or prejudice on bases of their 'Names' and 'Surnames' since they believe in the dilemma of regional 'Names' and 'Surnames'.

The 'Names' and 'Surnames' are just some titles we humans have learnt and use in our day to day life to picturise and avoid confusions and it has nothing to do with the divinity or copyright issue but the illogical mind finds it arduous to decipher that there is no such thing. There are many 'Names' and 'Surnames' in Goa which are very common but have no roots in Goa. Like for example the Surname *Naik* is not of Goan inception but a military designation found in King Shivaji's army. The Surname *Rane* is derived from the title *Ranas*, the rulers of Rajasthan who later migrated to Sanquelim & Sattari village. The Surname *Nayak* was the designation given to the Governors of the Vijayanagar province and the Surnames like *Aguiar, Alemao, Afonso, Barbosa, Lobo, Cardozo, Fernandes, Mascarenhas, Menezes, Vaz* are all Portuguese Titles given to the new converts of Goa. It is an equivocal expression that a Goan can be identified by his / her Names and Surnames. One cannot ignore the mischievous motive behind migrants transmuting their 'Names' and 'Surnames' in Goa and it needs to be taken under scrutiny. One of the few reasons that Migrants transmute their Names, Surnames is to evade the slang *"Ghati"* or *"Biknakaars"* referred to a non-Goan. If one states his Name as Shankar Mallappa or Rajput or Lamani or Patel than he is considered as "Ghaati" or "Biknakaar".

- *Carving out Good and Bad Migrants.*

The Goan economy is majorly dependent on the Tourism industry and it has benefited the natives who have set their businesses and offer their services near areas of tourist enticements. There are many native dwellers near beaches who have converted their house, flat and bungalow into a tourist accomodation. The natives largely depends on migrant worker and labour to provide services in their shacks eateries and other service establishments. There is no doubt that the migrant labour is adding value to the businesses and ecomonic pursuits.

- *Unemployment- the blame game*

It is improper to blame migrants for the growing unemployment figures of youth in Goa. First of all, there is high appetite for Government jobs among Goans. The preference for jobs in private sector is low. Private recruiters perceived difficulties in recruiting Goans. As the youth find private employment little "disagreeable". The "susegado" posture of Goans is erroneously messed up in the minds of recruiters as lack of commitment and responsibility.

- *Illegalities right under the nose*

Goa has become an incipient hub of illicit activities which include heinous malefaction like murders, rapes, prostitution, drug peddling, illicit selling and buying of land and carrying out business through illicit companies and enterprise. Natives claim that there has been an increase in crime rate in Goa solely because of migrants. Such accusations against migrants are missplaced. These are issuse of policing and low enforcement.

- *Vote Bank politics*

Migrants and weaker sections fall easy prey to politicians. It is not just migrants, but it is the underprivileged sections who are victims of vote bank politics. It is the insecurity of shelter and lack of access to public services that makes migrants vulnerable.

Conclusion

Goa has survived several assailants of communal and regional politics sustaining its secular character and the reason behind it is none other than the homogenous people of Goa irrespective of their caste, religion and ethnicity who have contributed directly or indirectly to the development and the sustenance of its distinctiveness and ethos.

It is pellucid that the engendered delusion of ethnic dilution among Goans has been the sole reason of dispute and abhorrence between Goans and Migrants which has effected the placid and secular notion of "Goemkarponn". These delusions are engendered intentionally to gain political mileage or to divide communities to organize vote banks.

There are many migrants whose children are educated and employed in Goa and have become part of Goan culture and tradition. Migration is a very old phenomenon and curbing migration is impossible.

Defining a Goan may be a facile task but to be one takes sheer dedication and commitment. The migrants who have settled in Goa have dedicatedly accepted the local culture, tradition and language. Their children go to state-run schools learning Konkani and Marathi and additionally top in these subjects. They have contributed to the economy and development, they have become a component of "Goemkarponn" and their identity as a Goan cannot be taken away.

The trepidation propagated that the Goan culture and identity will soon end because of migrants doesn't substantiate the present reality. Migration commenced long before the liberation of Goa. However, the Goan ethos never got washed away but were definitely embraced by the new settlers blending new colours to the same.

No doubt, migrants today are everywhere and in every field but they are just occupying the vacant spaces. No Goan will be obliged to work as a labour since majority of the youths are educated and aspire for good and better income opportunities. There is additionally this concept of white collar job which determines the reputation and respect of an individual.

The anti-migrant sentiment will engender only rifts in the society and perturb the inter-state relations. A 21-day lockdown in goa during covid pandemic proved how badly we are dependent on neighbouring states for supply of labour, vegetables and dairy products. There are many Goans who have migrated and settled to different neighbouring states and other parts of the world embracing a new culture and tradition, they never have been treated as a threat to those regions. The goggles of regional politics exhibits only threat and ethnic dilution but in reality, there has been a dilution of a zealous, secular and tolerant "Goemkarponn" from Goa.

Goans must ascend above all the divisions and dedicate their energy towards the development of Goa and fostering the liberalism and social harmony.

Making Peace with Migrants

History has proved that migrants build the economy of the region at a faster pace than what would have been possible for the local communities. In fact, the petition and requisition for the migrants is a derived demand. This demand springs from the goods and services provided by the migrants and needed by the locals in any region. Had it not been for this, any form of migration would not happen. The reasons for immigration into Goa are no different from the motives which account for the migration of locals to other territories. It is erroneous to assume that migration materialises due to the demand for voters and vote banks by political leaders and political parties. Labelling migrants as refugees and burden on local communities is a result of inadequate understanding. It is almost a culture amongst locals in Goa to single out migrants as the cause of the problems of Goan economy and society.

Migrants build, locals destroy

We expect migrants to serve the requirements of our economic and infrastructure development and dislike them almost nearing to the point of hate. We ridicule their unhygienic "ghettos" bordering every town in our state. We want them to serve our interests enhancing our quality of life. At the same time, our mind gets filled with thunder storms if migrants get access to basic needs of shelter, water, electricity, and identity cards for rations and voting.

The popular contention is that migrants destroy local environment and culture. Further, they pose a threat to identity due to demographic disturbance. In reality, this is far from truth. In fact, Migrants at the bottom of the ladder get assimilated into the culture, language and causes of the locals. They add value to economy as well as preservation of natural environment. If any harm amounting to destruction is visible, it needs to be attributed to the involvement and abetment by locals mainly belonging to the landed elite and political class. In any case, such damage could be caused even without immigration. It is wrong to pull the trigger on the head of the migrant.

Immediately after liberation of Goa, the human resource for primary and school education came from neighbouring states followed by human capital for government services and health sector. Now, we have local manpower in this area. With public investment in infrastructure, port development and urban services, there was dearth of labour which resulted in a flutter of migration. The real estate boom of the last two decades and the inappropriate choice of investments in industrial estates lured more migration. These migrants found Goa attractive and convenient for settlement and education of their children as compared to their places of origin. The migrants find the place better governed and relatively offering better access to basic human needs as compared to the regions of their birth. The small size of the state gives them access to centres of political and administrative power which is an elusive luxury in their hometowns and villages. In Goa, they find not only livelihood but a hope of enriching their daily lives and of their children.

From labour to petty entrepreneurship

In short, the migrants have built the tourism, housing and public works infrastructure of Goa. Their entry has not snatched opportunities of the locals since the entry of the less privileged migrants is in the area "unoccupied" by the locals. Locals lament that the real estate boom has thrown them out of the market. Undoubtedly true, but the anger of disenfranchisement from housing and real estate should not load up on the migrants. It is the marriage between the local property owners and the capital from outside that accounts for the loss-win situation. Goa's identity and environment, if at all it is destroyed, it can be only by the locals, nobody else.

There seems to be tolerance to non-local investors in land and real estate and business in the organised sector. The growing hold on business in the unorganised sector by non-locals raises eyebrows. The entry of migrants in the retail sector and wholesale business which traditionally has been a local fiefdom is a subject of prejudiced debate. These are areas where locals have shied away and exhibited unwillingness to get involved. It is pointless to accuse migrants for entering these areas since these are equally available for all. Today, entrepreneurship opportunities are visible in all petty trades and services. Finally, this serves the needs of the expanding markets. It is natural that the gaps in demand and supply would be filled from either internal or external source. These are market realities which we need to understand and digest rather than spitting fire at the migrants.

Nouveau locals not vote banks

The heat and the hate for migrants is seen at most of the locations. They are viewed as interrupters of development of locals and circuits which close identity and culture. Despite making the most desired contributions to the economy of the region, they are hunted as vote banks. It is a generally held belief that crime and anti-social activity is the pitch of the migrants. This thinking also forces the agenda of political parties. Regional political outfits get irrigated with the anti-migrant programme. This is seen in Goa as also in the neighbouring states. For their continued survival such outfits pump the fuel of dissent and discord in the community. Such a climate also forces migrants to look at politicians as protectors of their ramshackle dwellings and economic interests. This is the easy option open to migrants after they are disowned by the local community. The local media too plays the strings sending the vibes that the migrant population is the evil genie which needs to be bottled.

It is necessary to understand that migration and immigration are inevitable and would happen in all societies and regions primarily due to economic factors. Converting migrants into a political football is unfair and unjust. The war against migrants and particularly prejudice against those who are denied access to basic amenities and public services is uncharitable and inhuman.

Mujhe Ghar Jana Hai - the Covid fall out

(with inputs from Akbar Gaded)

Empty pockets, empty stomach, and fear of losing shelter including worry of their future employment prospects, the migrants stranded amidst Covid19 and politics had no option but to leave the state and somehow reach their home town. Migrants perpetually pleaded through news media, attempted to connect to their native government through video messages for help but it was least addressed. Struggling with economic expenditure and satisfying the Covid19 codes of conduct without any source of income during lockdown, even the state government soon realised it is failing to nurture the stranded people and their desperation to return home needs to be addressed. The Goa government made the decision and to its surprise, 80,000 migrants echoed their voice to return home. The outcome was the result of the lockdown experience and emotional trauma undergone by the migrant.

All Goa Bakers and Confectioners Association expressed concern that the labourers have already forsaken their employers and desired their wish to go to their domicile town. The Goa Chamber of Commerce and Industry (GCCI) urged the government to organize counselling measures for migrants to convince them to stay back to avoid labour shortage. In another breadth, the captains of business and industry also talked foul alleging that the migrant labour is moving out only to encash a free ride back home. Many Goans at home and those settled overseas could not resist their glee to castigate migrants as vote banks and as those who want to have the cake and eat it too.

Social media was rife with venom against the migrants for being given access to bare necessities and also for being provided with instruments such as ration card and Aadhar. This for many is the pampering of the migrant. When the state of Goa promulgated food packages to stranded migrants, the move was criticised by some sections on social media as endeavouring to appease migrant vote bank. When the government announced a relief to registered labourers under the "Goa Labour Welfare Board Assistance Scheme COVID-19", social media websites were flooded with critical and racist remarks calling the ruling Goa government "Ghatiyancho Sarkar". The furore escalated which made the Chief Minister to clarify that the monetary relief announced by labour and employment minister is availed by Goans only and not migrants.

"I appeal to labourers with folded hands. Don't pay heed to any rumours. It is the responsibility of the government to see that you get work at the place you were working.... don't take the hasty decision of going to your native place", said Karnataka Chief Minister BS Yediyurappa after a group of builders met him and communicated the fears of scarcity of labourers. Such appeals also came from the Chief Minister of Goa. The contractors and employers who deserted their labourers without wage and without any humane help were worried visualizing their industry with labour scarcity.

Migrants are known for their orientation to land and agriculture. Many of them own land but perceive no future. They see a future for their children in towns and cities. If the village economy can empower them, things can be different for the poor and less privileged.

This migrant exodus could cripple the Goan economy. The migrant population has been a source of relatively cheap labour. There are many industries, MSMEs and economic activities such as real estate, construction, carpentry, masonry, fisheries, public infrastructure works, cargo handling, beach shack operations, bakery, horticulture, solid waste management which are majorly dependent on migrant labour community. Paucity of labour would mean an operational paralysis for these sectors.

Migrants not only bring hands to work but also multiply the mouths to feed. Their consumption expenditure keeps the tempo in retail trade, petty businesses and informal economic sector. The purchasing power in the hands of the migrants is what results in the demand-push sustaining enterprises in villages and around the industrial estates. The children of migrants are sustaining the enrolment figures in rural and urban schools, otherwise deserted by the locals.

Covid-19 has brought to the fore the critical and substantive role of migrants in the economic development of the regions. It is a different matter that they are condemned for creating a home away from their native home and also damned for their return to their native lands. The entry of the migrant is marked by hate and unwelcome language. Their exit also invites similar reactions.

The pandemic times are also underlining the utter violation of labour welfare laws by corporate sector under the nose of the government. The quid pro quo migrants receive for their labour contribution is unfairly low. This is evident from the absence of their 'staying power' beyond a week. This is the state of all labour, whether local or migrant.

"Mujhe Ghar Jana Hai"----- will this figure a change in the craze for a shelter in the town which leaves the rural and village lands drained of human resources?

Goa & Goans: No Integration Deficit

Goans are not fully integrated into national mainstream. Some Goans are not emotionally and culturally integrated with India. I have been listening to such statements mainly from those who take pride in calling themselves as Rashtriya Swayam Sevaks and those Swatantra Sainiks whose minds are always in bondage. But of late, such views are being also expressed consistently by others plunging me into a national mainstream integration fatigue.

Why are Goans labelled as less integrated with the nation? Why at every given opportunity, we are told that some Goans still look at the erstwhile rulers? Will those some Goans be always branded as less Indian because of imbibed traits of Portuguese lifestyle, food style and dress style? What exactly is Indian culture and national mainstream? Is Goan culture not a part of Indian culture like that of Kerala, Maharashtra, Punjab or Gujarat? Is it not because of the culture and lifestyle of Goans that Goa is a jewel of India? Has not Goa given the opportunity to the nation to internationally boast of a space cosmopolitan in outlook and yet providing the purity and tranquillity of the village?

It is time to put a full stop to this dirty game of questioning the national integrity of Goans, though referred to as "those few or those some" at regular intervals. Nobody is naïve not to understand the community singled out for reference. Is a Goan Christian in any way less Indian?

I have heard many saying that Christians prefer to migrate overseas. But, what has this to do with assimilation into the national mainstream? Community wise statistics of migration of Goans would not show much difference in recent years. We will also find same results if we document migration from Punjab, Maharashtra, Gujarat, South Karnataka and Delhi.

It is very easy to use the cultural baton to project cultural alienation of specific groups or communities. But, we are neither a mono-cultural society nor our culture is static and rigid. Culture cannot be reckoned on basis of isolated bits of behaviour. I read the news that a Christian was cremated as per Hindu customs as per the wish of the individual. The pracharaks who equate and bind Indian culture to only Hindu traditions, customs, and rituals immediately equated this to patriotism and nationalism. A few weeks back, the dead body of a freedom fighter was donated to the medical college. This behaviour has still not come in the statute books of Bharatiya culture! The fanatics may even consider this as an affront on culture!

People who talk about Goans or any communities as having not totally mingled into Indian culture or mainstream should first learn to understand culture. Jawaharlal Nehru in his Glimpses of World History says "Culture and civilisation are difficult to define, and I shall not try to define them. But among the many things that culture includes are, certainly restraint over oneself and consideration of others. If a person has not got this self-restraint and has no consideration for others, one can certainly say that he is uncultured."

Look at the conflicting and multiple stands on the film 'Arakshan' by Prakash Jha who is known for a socialist tilt. Some States have chosen to ban the film. Some groups of the Scheduled Castes feel that the contents are harsh on them. There are groups of the forward castes also demanding a ban on the film since the contents are unfair to them. Look at how a painting of M. F. Husain created a controversy and look at how he was hunted, that he had to quit the nation and die in a foreign territory. Examine for yourself small outfits like the Shiv Sena, who do not have power beyond some municipal limits of Maharashtra, parade themselves as repositories of national mainstream and culture. Go back to the days of the infamous riots in Gujarat and Mumbai and draw your own lessons on what is our mainstream and our culture. I remember the Vishwa Hindu Parishad making it loud and clear that they will not listen to the Supreme Court but to the scriptures! It is not that such things are not said by religious fanatics in other communities. Goans have witnessed the explosions and turmoil created by the 'sadaks' of Sanathan Saunstha, which professes to be the outfit of nationalism and culture. All this is a mirror of what the nation is. All this reflects on what we are. It is the cultural growth of the future that will teach us to make cultured choices.

I have to put on record a note of caution to all Goans mainly due to the use and abuse of the internet communication by overseas Goans. Their best recreation is talking about Goa and how it should be kept pure and pristine. I read a tweet from such a foreigner who prefers to show off as Goan 'Goa is a place where Goans are just 29% of the total population'. This is indirectly suggesting that only Christians are pure Goans. The word of caution here is to avoid blaming the Christian community in Goa for such outbursts by foreigners. These outbursts are because of the guilt feeling of losing the roots. I also find outbursts from Hindus who have accepted foreign citizenship. They turn irrational and adore superstitions as culture. This could be because they live in guilt and a complex for embarcing a foreign land. To prove, their Indianess, it is this overseas Hindu community which provides liberal funding to religious outfits in India to propagate the archaic practices, unscientific traditions and discriminatory beliefs as Indian culture. Probably, it is their way of negotiating their fears and testifying their Indianess. Some may consider donations as atonement of sins as their children have migrated to foreign lands, leaving their lands of their Gods and deities. They want to enjoy the fruits of liberal societies and developed economies. At the same time, they give a thumbs-up for Indian society to stay primitive, sunk in blind faith.

When we ourselves cannot define the mainstream culture, we should not single out the Goan community all the time. If culture means our behaviour with others, if culture means rejecting discriminatory practices and adopting progressive values, if culture also includes universal values, then Goa and Goans is a storehouse for the national mainstream to draw to its kitty.

Nobody can deny these two unique natural traits in a Goan's lifestyle. To share, care and love others without expectation. In other parts of India, you may find this only in remote villages and hilly regions. The next is a non-bothering attitude. That's why you will not find Goans creating any ruckus over a visit of a film star or politician. Each one can get his private space. As I conclude, let me also say that these identity traits are not free from attack.

The Last Word

> *Nothing could be more religious for Goans than its social harmony.*

The struggle against projects on highly plausible grounds of ecology, environment and the imminent threat of converting this tiny land into a mere transit destination for coal is an authentic issue. The attempt to push the argument of Goa for Goans kills the merits of such movements and adulterates the valid issues which are of economic, environmental and ecological nature. Banners and kites of 'persons of Goan origin' (POGO) and exhorting locals to get prepared for a 'revolution' are attractive and spicy theoretical propositions. They keep a miniscule slice of locals residing in the tiny State and some few residing overseas or falling in the bracket of "overseas citizens of India" charged with this opium of insiders and outsiders.

It is a tested observation that when economic activity slips from the hands of locals, the tendency for political leaders is to release the insider and outsider balloons in the political skies by refilling the gas of the so-called rich tradition and distinct culture. Concerns about the local language get echoed at different forums. Changing technology, advances in communications, economic liberalization and opportunities of migration will definitely shape a new culture and life-style. The issue to be addressed is of business, commerce, skills and employment but all subjects unrelated to economics are brought to the centre stage along with a subtle hate campaign against immigrants. This anti-migrant tobacco chewing by locals serves no purposeful agenda of growth and development; neither has it contributed to the resurrection of language, identity and culture. It elevates politicians to the status of protectors of both migrants and locals. People get compartmentalized into vote banks and small interest-groups espousing what according to them are the most significant public causes. As it is, there are divisions on basis of religion and caste. These get compounded with partitions of language and culture. In this bargain, the locals tend to lose economics, land and economy. They tend to cling to something which is ephemeral.

As we open the curtain of the State politics, we see the dance of democracy directed by political defections. The BJP has converted politics and democracy into some kind of casino gambling throughout the country. Narendra Modi's BJP is the all-time ready buyer and neurotic engineer of defections. Every activity is infested with the bug of entertainment. We see these microbes of entertainment damaging big sporting events like cricket and football. These germs have permeated in print and electronic media. The media can no longer lay claims to be the fourth estate. The print journalist had donned the shoes of an entertainer and the anchors on TV screens resembles jesters. Social media is emerging as the leading manufacturer and distributor of fake news and communication. The entertainment bacteria are eating into the vitals of sports, art, music, films, theatre and other performing arts.

"**Neighbour's envy, owner's pride**", is how Goans hold Goa in their minds and hearts irrespective of whether they reside in their small tiny paradise or worldwide. Apart from the rich natural gifts which 'amchem goem' abounds, what stands out as Goa's identity is the proverbial social harmony and the free mix between communities. Goans are known worldwide for liberal thought and respect to free choices of individuals. A non-bothering attitude and a contented lifestyle is what distinguishes a Goan from the rest.

This tiny land on the West coast of India, admeasuring 3702sqm and a population of 14.59 lakh is in fact the laboratory and library of peaceful co-existence for the rest of India to emulate. The community of Goans is a positive example where diversity of religions, languages, faith, worship, dress, food and music are celebrated. For a Goan, Goa and preservation of its unique social harmony comes first. Partaking and involving in each other's community festivals is an established tradition. Instances of a Goan turning mad and fundamental on issues of faith and religion are indeed very rare. No doubt, Goans are religious but it has never caused eruptions in public discourse. The practice of religion has not produced narrowness, intolerance and irrationalism despite the machinations of politicians and groups with fundamentalist leanings.

Having said this, it needs to be underscored that the current situation is disturbing and a cause for concern. Though, Goa has not lost its prized seat of peace and social harmony, the current track could take us to the final destination of intolerance and communal discord. It is therefore necessary to understand the forces which are sowing and nurturing the seeds of insecurity, distrust and discord and their motivations. Together with this, we should be prepared with a corrective to arrest the ugly designs of these evil forces.

It is not that Goa was free from the games of organizations with communal intent and similar acts of vested interest groups. Attempts to lure a social division and maintain an atmosphere of tension between the two major communities in Goa by invoking the dead skeletons of the infamous Goa Inquisition always existed and still exists. These same forces practice their evil "dharma" of making derogatory references to St. Francis Xavier who is revered as 'Goencho Saib'. The threat of religious conversions is another instrument used to multiply inter-community suspicions. Earlier, such attempts were feeble and done stealthily in hiding fearing disgrace. Today, these are done with great pomp and pride and paraded as acts of nationalism. Politicians from right-wing ideology are irrigating these forces today with the clear objective to polarize the people on communal lines. With political patronage, such destructive forces are gaining monetary resources, muscle and media gaze to spread discord. They also get projected as crusaders and saviors of national culture.

The BJP party is known to pedal Hindutva as nationalism. The job of raising the bogey of Hindu Rashtra is allocated to the frontal organizations. We have seen in Goa, a communal spectacle being designed and created over the issue of the statute of the Marathi warrior Shivaji. The BJP government is keen on rewriting history and correcting what it considers to be the historical wrongs during the colonial rule in Goa. This is directed to embolden the divisive forces by igniting false sense of national pride. The end objective seems to be to inject in people, the pride in their faith and prepare them to break each other's heads.

The movement towards a modern, cultured and scientific society is associated with the shift from sentiment to reason in public discourses and public affairs. However, we observe a reversal of this scenario when communalism and fundamentalism take charge of the thinking minds. Outdated traditions and obsolete practices in respect of caste and gender get bolstered as sentiment overpowers reason and rational social thinking.

Hate speech of any kind was unheard in Goa. Today, it is an innovation to gloat in religious and caste pride. Hate speech is getting political patronage and also the silent consent of the educated, the rich industry magnates, the respectable professionals and the bold and beautiful from showbiz.

Goa, which should have been the laboratory of fraternity for the rest of India to follow, is itself being converted into a ground of inter-community hate and discord. As if the state and non-state actors within Goa were not enough, new imports are descending on this land of peace and harmony.

It is good to be religious but it is horror to take pride in faith, the way organized religion and BJP politicians exhort the followers. Religion is respectable only in the form of moral values but dangerous with the added content of superstition, violence and exploitation. Post-2014, we observe that elections are fought on robust nationalism. The ruling BJP, the frontal organizations of the BJP and the right-wing actors tend towards focusing the people's sentiments on religion, nationalism and culture. We observe in Goa, the Chief Minister and the BJP raking up dead issues with references to colonial rule and colonial wrongs. This is to incite communal emotions. Every issue whether it is as mundane as erecting a statue of Shivaji Maharaj is aimed to ensure a communal divide and polarization of the people on religious lines. It's time to be wise not to fall prey to the dirty designs. Nothing could be more religious for Goans than its social harmony. Equally important is to guard the liberal life style and the freedom of choice, expression and creativity of the majority community.

Printed in the USA
CPSIA information can be obtained
at www.ICGtesting.com
CBHW022137011024
15215CB00059B/2568

9 789358 983715